FOUCHÉ, THE MAN NAPOLEON FEARED

FOUCHÉ

From a painting by J. L. David

FOUCHÉ
THE MAN
NAPOLEON FEARED

BY

NILS FORSSELL

Translated from
the Swedish by

ANNA BARWELL

AMS PRESS
NEW YORK

Reprinted from the edition of 1928, New York
First AMS EDITION published 1970
Manufactured in the United States of America

SBN: 404-02514-5
Library of Congress Catalog Card Number: 71-112299

AMS PRESS, INC.
NEW YORK, N.Y. 10003

FOREWORD

THE name of Joseph Fouché is intimately and inextricably connected with the important period of the French Revolution and the Napoleonic era. Just as his career is impressed throughout by the great events of the time, so it bears, to a very great degree, plain marks of his own will. For Fouché has not only, like many others, filled important posts during the heroic age of the Republic in the stern Reign of Terror, through the Directoire with its plots and intrigues, the Consulate régime of inner equilibrium and outward brilliance, the Empire's formal splendour, the errors and defeat of the " hundred days ", and lastly the desperate Government of the second Restoration—a record which is in itself no slight proof of political adaptability—but he was also one of those who exercised influence and power in the mighty movements of this long and ever-changing drama.

It is true that Fouché but seldom crosses the stage in the full glare of the footlights. But if we fix our attention on the decisive turning-points in the course of events, we discover him at last, much as we see the details appear on the dark background of a negative in process of development. For in the background appears little by little a tall, thin, angular figure, an impenetrable face, pale as death, with eyes that avoid our glance. We meet him behind the scenes in the Convention Hall when the sands of Robespierre's dictatorship are running low. At the *Brumaire coup* we catch a glimpse of him

7

again, as an essential fellow-actor, even though he takes no prominent part on the stage. At the establishment of the Empire he is busy in some out-of-the-way corner as an indispensable stage-manager. He works in silence for Napoleon's divorce of Josephine, and it is accomplished, too, in due season. After a few years' absence he suddenly makes his reappearance in 1815 at the very centre of events, though even now half-invisible in the background. Napoleon fights against his hidden influence as against a secret, inevitable fate. Then at last Fouché ventures out into the sunshine, and for a moment takes the helm to steer the ship of state into the port of the renewed power of the Bourbons. But this figure, like the fairy-tale hobgoblins, seems unable to bear the light of day; he is pushed back again from his place in the foreground and disappears for ever into the twilight.

A hasty glance then at the vicissitudes of Fouché's life seems to show us its varying activities as dark and lacking brilliance, yet important and engrossing to the highest degree. His work throughout was a silent but obstinate and remorseless struggle to keep himself afloat through the changing currents of the time. And such a fight often means life or death, or, at all events, influence or impotence. And in such case it may only too easily happen that the accepted rules of human life are broken and fail under the strain of suffering, whilst the primitive instinct of self-preservation brutally tramples beneath its feet all the laws of humanity and consideration for others. It is said that in deep water there is sometimes no way of escape from the convulsive grip of a drowning man other than ruthlessly to free oneself from his grasp and let him sink to the bottom. Is that right or wrong? Is that using more violence than necessity requires? To such questions as these there often seems no answer. At all events, the distant onlooker finds it difficult to give a just verdict in such a test of strength. Thus prudence bids us use discretion in pronouncing judgment on such a man as Joseph Fouché in his efforts to work his way through the restless tumult of his time. The measure of his guilt is and will remain, in any case, full enough and to spare.

But if we are interested in trying to understand the connecting force underlying the many changes in Fouché's life and his course of action, we must begin by dwelling on his years of training in the shelter of the Oratorian Order and on his unhappy début in politics during the days of the Revolutionary Reign of Terror. For there alone shall we find the key to his exceedingly dramatic and exciting career.

It only remains to add that after the Swedish edition of this book was published in 1925, it was submitted by me to a complete revision with reference to more recent literature on the subject. It is, of course, evident that, however extensive my list of sources, it cannot claim to be entirely exhaustive when it is a question of dealing with the enormous mass of Napoleonic literature. I can only state that use has been made of all the most important material.

NILS FORSSELL.

CONTENTS

PART II

FOUCHÉ, NAPOLEON AND LOUIS XVIII

CONTENTS

XXI.   THE COLLAPSE OF THE EMPIRE AND THE RULE OF THE
         BOURBONS   208

         Fouché's holocaust of papers—In banishment—In Dresden,
         1813—The Illyrian Provinces—Murat—Fouché and the
         first Restoration—Conspiracies.

XXII. THE " HUNDRED DAYS " AND THE SECOND
         RESTORATION   218

         Fouché against Napoleon and the Bourbons—These wish
         to arrest him—His flight—Becomes Napoleon's Minister
         of Police—Deceives him—Fouché winds up the " Second
         Empire "—Louis XVIII's valued servant—His aristocratic
         marriage—Treachery to, and fight for, the revolutionary
         cause—His final fall.

XXIII. FOUCHÉ'S EXILE AND DEATH   232

         Fouché proscribed—His loss of self-control in exile—A
         roué of the Revolution—Prague, Lenz and Trieste—Calm
         after storm—Death—Dramatic burial—Fouché's survivors.

XXIV. THE VERDICT OF POSTERITY   238

         A forceful nature—Guardian of the Revolution legacy—
         Napoleon's Minister—The traitor—Before and after 1799
         —The Convention's Representative on Mission—The ideal
         of the Intellectual Movement as against Nationalism—
         Fouché as an historical personality—The toiler on the sea.

XXV.   SOURCES OF INFORMATION CONCERNING FOUCHÉ . 248

         Biographies and biographical studies—Printed and unprinted
         documents—Memoirs—Epitomes and special works.

         INDEX   254

ILLUSTRATIONS

ILLUSTRATIONS

PART I

FOUCHÉ AND THE FRENCH REVOLUTION

Chapter I

Breton and Oratorian

" LA mer est si grande et ma barque est si petite "
(" The sea so great, so small my boat ! ") is the refrain
of an old Breton folksong whose notes may well have
resounded beside the cradle of Joseph Fouché, for he
first opened his eyes to the light of day in Brittany on
the little holding of Pellerin, not far from Nantes, whilst
his father was a sea-captain and his forefathers, for many
generations back, seafaring folk.   The sense of the im-
mensity of the ocean and of man's insignificance when
face to face with natural forces, so vast as to be beyond
all human calculation, may well have made a deep
impression at a very early age upon the sensitive mind
of a young child.   But the constant sight of the sea
not only suggested thoughts and fancies to his mind,
but presented to his eyes as well the picture of the sailor's
struggle with the raging elements and of his skill in furl-
ing his sails against the storm, in scudding along before
a favourable wind and tacking in the contrary breezes.
A sharp eye, a steady hand on the tiller and imperturbable
calm in all weathers were, every one of them, qualities
that seem to have been included in Joseph Fouché's
birthright.   It is true that his restless life later on led
him far from the scenes of his childhood, yet possibly
in all life's hurly-burly he may have followed the signs
and portents that had in earlier times guided his father
as he sailed amidst the fogs and sandbanks of the English

Channel and through the surging billows of the Atlantic Ocean. Perhaps the bold sailor, with but a frail plank separating him from the vast silence of the ocean depths, and the political navigator, steering his course with unflinching energy through the wild tumults of human life and the critical phases and upheavals of the Napoleonic era—perhaps, after all, both alike possessed the same hard yet supple hand, the same invincible calm, and the same indomitable instinct of self-preservation that kept the one no less than the other safely afloat on the face of the mighty deep.

Fouché's father was a well-to-do man, who, in addition to Pellerin, owned plantations in San Domingo and several properties in his native Brittany, from one of which his son in his younger days was known as Joseph Fouché of Rouzerolles. At the age of ten the boy was boarded in Nantes and his name entered as a scholar in a preparatory school there, belonging to the Order of the Oratorians, no doubt with the idea that he would shortly decide to devote himself to a sailor's life such as his father's.

But Fate willed otherwise. Joseph Fouché was small and thin, a delicate lad with a weak voice and a weak chest, and how could such a son follow in his father's footsteps? But unfortunately he seemed to have little liking for study either, and, writing of his youthful days, he tells us that his first teachers regarded him with but little favour. His gaiety was accounted superficiality, dry grammatical study gave him no pleasure, and he tried in vain to solve the mysteries of Latin and French verse. This was a serious flaw, for a good translation was in itself considered by the Oratorians a crowning

20

proof of ability, as we learn from Lallemand's history of their system of education. But the precepts of the Order not only required the teacher to fix the pupils' standard of acquirement, but also to study their characters and endeavour to guide them to a goal which seemed suitable to each one's natural gifts. The Principal of the school at Nantes, Durif by name, soon noticed that in free times, when his school-fellows were devouring tale-books, Fouché was absorbed in the study of Pascal, whose writings he had found in the library. Durif then began to talk with Fouché on these difficult and abstract subjects, and, to his astonishment, found his pupil quite able to grasp them. But probably it was Pascal as the *mathematician* rather than the gifted *philosopher* that had attracted Fouché; at any rate he relates that now he "was studying mathematics and making progress in them".

His father had already died when it was decided to give him further training for the teaching profession at the Oratorians' Paris seminary, situated in Rue St. Honoré, and there, on December 1, 1781, he began his studies at the age of twenty-two. The Oratorian Order had been marked by its distinctly religious character from the very first, when it was founded in 1611 by the pious Pierre de Berulle to combat the unbelief which had become general in France after the destructive dissensions that had rent the Church about the year 1500, and which had assumed an attitude of downright hostility to Christianity as the result of the Renaissance with its devotion to classic art. The Order was purely ecclesiastical, and its members were under an obligation not to take monastic vows. Its educational institutions were to be found all over France, and were most highly prized by the upper classes. Their aim was to combat by gentle means even in childhood natural instincts and every form of egoism, and then, having destroyed the old man, to create a new creature endowed with all Christian virtues. This aim was identical with that of the Jansenists, another ecclesiastical body, with whom they had much sympathy and many points in common. Saint-Cyran, one of the earlier members of this body, had in his time declared that the little child who, when playing with his brother, catches sight of an apple, and divides it unequally to get the best piece, gives proof of the germ that will later develop into the passionate man, and when that child later on catches sight of opportunities of power he will in like manner seize them, saying : These I take and keep henceforth to the very end. The great and only means of conquering man's inveterate original sin, and indeed the only path to freedom from the body of sin, was, according to the Jansenists and Oratorians, devotion to Christ, whose grace alone redeems lost human nature. The expression of their conviction is set forth by the great Swedish poet, Carl David of Wirsén, in his stanzas on Port-Royal, the stronghold of Jansenism :—

> The darker the shadow, the brighter the dawn,
> Each moment imbued with a breath of eternity.

There may indeed seem something grotesque in speaking of the sublime traditions of Port-Royal in connection with Joseph Fouché, that practised and inveterate sinner in all phases of public life, the man who, to the very last, with immoral persistency stretched out eager hands for the golden fruit of power. But the fact remains that twenty years of Fouché's life were passed within the setting of the Oratorian Order. And, therefore, if we wish to find the various factors that played their part in his development and the distinctive influences that decided his conduct, we must pause to consider his training and activity as a member of this Order. And in so doing we shall find that the contradictions between school and scholar are not so pronounced as one might think.

Fouché himself relates that he soon wearied of the seminary studies of the Catholic catechism as drawn up at the Council of Trent and of the theological subtleties of the teacher, Jansenius. He was more interested in authors such as Tacitus—possibly the attraction here being the writer's incisive descriptions of the licentious and depraved characters of imperial Rome—or Horace, the worldly satirist, or in Euclid, that first classic exponent of inevitable conclusions, certain data having been given. There is little reason to challenge Fouché's statements as to the precocious tastes that foreshadowed in so marked a way the part he was to play in later years. He begged, indeed, one of his teachers, the Abbé Mérault de Moissy, for counsel as to his private studies, and was advised to read, amongst others, two religious writers, the Jansenist Nicole and Jean Baptiste Massillon, one of the great preachers of the time of Louis XIV. In after years his connection with Mérault became one of Fouché's dearest memories of his youth. " His angelic soul won mine ", he wrote to a friend when an exile in 1816. And with even greater astonishment we read : " These were years filled with feelings of sweet delight, of true spiritual uplifting ".

To appraise such statements at their true value, we must, however, bear in mind that about 1780 the standard of spirituality demanded by the Oratorian Order was far less severe than that of an earlier period. In all social contests the Oratorians had always assumed a somewhat advanced and nonconforming attitude, accentuated by their chronic opposition to the Jesuits. After the latter body had been expelled from France in 1762, the days of trial and strife were at an end for the present, as far as the Jansenists and Oratorians were concerned, and this sense of peace was undoubtedly accompanied by an increase in worldliness. Their educational work was emphasized, whilst their religious duties were pushed into the background; they took part fearlessly in criticism of prevailing conditions, and who knows but that possibly under the existing circumstances an intelligence such as Fouché's, opposed to the actual facts of life, was able to draw conclusions even from the Jansenist Nicole's writings that might prove dangerous to the feudal character of French society, weakened as it already was in 1700. Such feudalism formed indeed a sharp contrast to the Jansenist ideal, the illusion of the first assembly of nothing but brothers and equals before Christ, in whom they lived and had their being. Did not teaching like this demand enmity towards the Catholic priesthood, which had exchanged spirituality for an ever-increasing worldliness, and that intervened with all its power between the individual and his God ? But even his study of Massillon could incite Fouché to criticism, for Massillon, so Brunetière asserts, was fond

24

of speaking of God as " the origin of nature " and as
" the Highest of all ", judging between oppressing kings
and oppressed people.   And finally, we must not unduly
exaggerate the obligations assumed by Fouché, as an
Oratorian, to the Church.   He never took the priestly
vows, but only those of *les ordres mineurs* and the position
of teacher in the Society.

But although the Oratorian Order did not imbue
Fouché with any conservative ideals, yet his work as
teacher exerted a profound influence upon him.   He
taught at Niort till October 1783, at Saumur till October
1784, Vendôme till September 1787, Juilly, outside Paris,
till the spring of 1788, Arras till October 1790, and at
Nantes until the dissolution of the Oratorian Order in
May 1792.   These were years of methodical order and
concentrated work, punctuated by courses of lectures
and time-tables, and only interrupted by much-needed
holidays spent in no less methodical rest at his ancestral
home of Pellerin.   Years, too, that made a deep impression
upon Fouché, for in his private life he always continued
to be the Oratorian, who was never swept into the
stream of dissipation and enjoyment either during the
revolutionary upheaval or the life of the Imperial Court.
The delicate little teacher was a precocious youth, with
a brain that quickly registered without effort his observations in the schoolroom and exercised supreme control
over subjects of study, conversation and outward
behaviour.   His class meantime offered a fruitful field
for psychological experiment and observation, for was
it not his duty to guide every pupil to the goal most
fitted to his natural gifts ?   Thus Fouché tested on
living, growing material the theories which he had

formulated concerning human vices, passions and dreams. Moreover, taken as a whole, there is always a decided touch of the pedagogue in Fouché's dry yet not unkindly sarcasm, and in the unfailing deliberation with which he met even the smallest of life's happenings. He is calm in storm, and ready with the least expenditure of force to deal with disturbing situations, and by a wise admixture of pardon and punishment to restore order once more. If at last we ask how this man with his delicate physique was able to endure the constant upheavals of this terrible time and to survive its unceasing storms, we shall perhaps find the most credible answer in the great help of the regular methodical work that upheld Fouché through fair and foul weather, and never failed to steady his estimate of favourable prospects and risks.

Of the many personal associations that Fouché made, there was never one that he willingly dropped. It has been noticed that a constant feature of Fouché's personal policy was never to make enemies, for in his opinion nothing was so calculated to complicate and envenom any situation as feelings and prejudices of so unreasonable and inexplicable a nature. On one occasion he himself cast a more favourable light upon this personal trait by declaring that nothing could be more contemptible than to allow changes of fortune to affect personal relationships. As examples we may quote Antoine Jay, his pupil at Niort, who afterwards for many years served him as his faithful secretary and correspondent. Again, in Vendôme one of his colleagues was d'Hauterive, who, as a prominent official in the department of Foreign Affairs during the Napoleonic era, rendered Fouché important services. A former pupil of his in Juilly, who in 1793 was found to be badly compromised in the Lyons rebellion against the Republic, was saved from the guillotine by the Convention Representative Fouché. And one other name must be mentioned in this connection—the Latin scholar, Billaud-Varennes, at that time master of the art of turning out elegant Latin verse, but during the Reign of Terror—to use Danton's epithet—the man " with the dagger under his tongue ", i.e. his sharp, summary retorts, the man who was more ready than his companions in the Committee of Public Safety to sign his name to the never-ceasing flood of death decrees. With Robespierre, too—whom Billaud and Fouché were in fullness of time to unite in sending to the headsman's axe—the latter became acquainted in Arras, where Robespierre was the Oratorians' lawyer, and Fouché, who had a good position with his inherited means, provided him with money in 1789 when he had to set out as deputy to the States General—a delicate undertaking, for Robespierre did not wish to be under an obligation to anyone nor to allow personal feelings to affect in any way the honesty of his personal judgment. Through this connection with Robespierre, Fouché also became acquainted with his sister Charlotte, who was evidently enchanted with Fouché's ease of manner, for she afterwards spoke without any reserve of his " attractive person and extreme amiability ". Possibly both she and her stern brother may have felt annoyed with Fouché as time passed without any formal suing on his part for Charlotte's hand. He, however, by no means forgot her, and procured a pension for her during Napoleon's time. We need only add that in

27

Arras Fouché came into touch with the officer of the fortification there, Carnot, who in later years was his fellow-actor in so many political dramas, and that one of his fellow-teachers there was Maurice Gaillard, later on his colleague for several years, to show that Fouché's friendships bore fruit in his after-life. These personal acquaintances certainly indicate in some measure the part Fouché was to play in the coming revolution, but they cannot of themselves be considered an incontestable proof that his radical period had then begun. As late as 1787 Billaud-Varennes was paying homage in sickly verse to King Louis XVI, and Robespierre, at about the same time, was lauding Henry IV in well-turned phrases as the father of his people. These are items that help to show the sudden fatality with which immediately afterwards the wave of revolution swept over the whole of French national life. We do, however, find an unmistakable point of contact with his later career in Fouché's intellectual interests.

Chapter II

*Fouché, the Intellectual Movement
and the Outbreak of Revolution*

IN the Juilly school, near Paris, Fouché found an opportunity for the freer development of his individuality as a teacher, for there he was responsible for the higher teaching in mathematics and physics, optional courses that became popular amongst the scholars. He took a special interest in the balloon experiments that became the rage after the trials carried out by the brothers Montgolfier in Annonay in 1783 ; in Arras he continued his efforts in this direction, and also interested himself in the mechanism of lightning-conductors. In 1791 Fouché accomplished a balloon ascent at Nantes which attracted general attention. Everywhere he worked with the greatest zeal to secure good equipment and upkeep of the physical laboratories.

But although physics were Fouché's chief interest during these years of his life, we have also reason to assume that the theories of natural science, which became increasingly prevalent in general thought during the eighteenth century, made the deepest impression upon him too. It became customary to treat with scorn the belief that the universe revolved round man as its self-evident centre. Astronomers, indeed, revealed in endless perspective a vast host of mighty heavenly bodies, each moving in its own particular path. Not only did man shrink in an appalling way as he stood against this imposing background, but his form was destroyed, on the other hand, when the microscope brought to light an endless host of infinitesimal living creatures, which until then had been utterly unknown. In face of these observations none of the old standards seemed to hold good, and everything had to submit to the humiliating law of comparison.

A bitter but telling commentary of these discoveries appeared about the same time in Swift's accounts of Gulliver's travels, which bring the hero alternately into touch with giants and dwarfs, and set forth human qualities either in hideous exaggeration or comical miniature. Thus Swift's classic work is in reality a ruthless application of the new discoveries in the sphere of natural science to human existence—a point of view certainly worthy of the attention of modern research. It was a time of irreverent observation of human nature no less than of the universe itself, and things were boldly called by their right names, regardless of sentiment or prejudice. But no matter how motley and varied the aspects under which life might appear, it was everywhere ruled by the law of causality, the same causes unfailingly producing identically the same results. Man's strength and greatness lie in the fact that, insignificant and earth-bound as he may be, yet with his power of logical thought he can also pierce the darkness of the innermost recesses of the universe and direct his flight to far horizons and new perspectives. This was the intellectual movement's manly pride and passion, its religion, if you will, somewhat frost-bitten maybe by the cool breath of common sense, yet ardent in its faith in the dawn of a happier time as the earnest of the progress of human development. It is certain that Fouché sensed something of this eighteenth-century enthusiastic confidence in the dawning triumphs and progress of man's development when he, time after time, started off in the car of his balloon amidst the unceasing cheers of enthusiastic crowds. It can scarcely have been a mere coincidence that, at this first entrance upon a wider political stage in the autumn of 1792, he should at once have ranged himself beside Condorcet, the great apostle of the idea of man's unceasing advance in the upward march of civilization.

But for the time, thoughts and convictions diametrically opposed to each other continued to live peacefully side by side within the framework of the old French feudalism, a condition of things described in Comte de Ségur's picturesque words as : " Liberty and monarchy, aristocracy and democracy, prejudice and reason, novelty and philosophy all united to bless our days, and never did a more terrible awakening follow a sweeter sleep and even more seductive dreams." In cruder fashion, this state of things has been compared with an attempt to combine a free Press such as exists in London with a despotism such as formerly existed in Tsarist Petersburg. The lighted fuse was laid near the powder magazine, and an explosion was bound to follow. A well-known Swedish historian, Harald Hjärne, regards the situation in France in a more realistic way when he characterizes the monarchy as " sick to the very top ", with eyes blinded to the necessity of making its authority really felt by the new tendencies and powers fighting within the nation. Ideas of the supreme might of the people were now gaining the ascendancy, and those in authority, without a struggle, allowed the power to be snatched out of their hands until a political anarchy followed, a fight of all against all. It was impossible not to see that forcible measures were essential if the State was not to be destroyed. Thus France was literally born again during the bitter experiences of the Revolution. Hjärne's views as to the causes and course of the French Revolution have been summarized here because in various details they reflect the opinion that Fouché himself held in his later years on these points. Even granting that Fouché's ideas were in some measure developed as a defence of his own share in the work of the Revolution, they still bear the stamp of the practical experience which he afterwards gained in the service of the State. Can we not imagine his contempt for the political blunderers at the Court of Louis XVI when we remember the demoniacal skill with which, as Napoleon's Minister of the Police, he mastered the art of exorcizing those unruly spirits who disturbed the life of the State? On December 24, 1816, he wrote in fact to the Duc de Richelieu, at that time French Foreign Minister : " None but a simpleton believes that political revolutions are the result of plots and the work of separate individuals. Those whom they strike are often their originators, and those who appear to be their leaders are but following the stream." This, at any rate, is half true. Fouché undoubtedly had much to answer for as regards the part he played in the Reign of Terror, and the whole of that period was certainly marked by political extravagances; none the less, however, it is true that the policy of the French monarchy proved at last weak and ineffectual. Louis XVI without question challenged the Third Estate when, at the meeting of the States General in the early summer of 1789, he plainly espoused the cause of the nobility and clergy, an act of imprudence that was shown to have been a political error when his efforts to subdue the rising in Paris proved unsuccessful. In his striking weakness he heaped misfortune after misfortune upon the royal cause by the obstinacy with which he fought for the privileges of the clergy, and at last brought about his own irrevocable defeat by his intimate alliance with foreign rulers against his own refractory subjects. This was the drama that Fouché's clear vision undoubtedly perceived from his horizon in Arras and Nantes. Even if his sympathies had not been with the friends of freedom, he would scarcely, "opportunist" that he was, have thrown in his lot with the losing side.

In its way it is significant of Fouché's career that he did not take any active part in politics during the early years of the Revolution. The happy feeling of brotherhood and re-creation which pervaded the active reforms and activities of the first constituent National Assembly was kindled, glowed and died away far from him. The nation's jubilant shouts resounding round the white steed of Lafayette, the head of the National Guard, fell in but muffled tones upon Fouché's ears. It was not until clouds began to lour over the path of the Revolution, not until that path led ever deeper into thorns and thistles, not until the day of the Reign of Terror, that iron age of hard, prosaic fact, began to dawn, that Fouché appeared upon the scene. But then, indeed, there was truth in the verdict that Lafayette himself had

pronounced in June 1793 to his friend the Princesse
d'Hénin : " The people's cause is no less dear to me,
I would give it my blood drop by drop, I would
count as lost every moment of my life that was not
devoted to this cause and to this alone, but—the charm
has gone."

Chapter III

Agitator in Nantes

ONLY a few words are still needed to explain how Fouché was brought into direct contact with the revolutionary policy before we pass on to his history under the Convention.

As we have seen, it was part of the Oratorians' liberal traditions to sympathize with the work of reform now beginning. At the church in Rue St. Honoré, in Paris, a mass was said for those revolutionaries who had met their death in the storming of the Bastille on that memorable July 14, 1789. In Arras enthusiasm ran high in the institution where Fouché was teaching; he suggested that a deputation should be allowed to go to offer allegiance to the National Assembly. It is true that the authorities of the Order forbade any such proceeding, but one of Fouché's colleagues, Daunou, afterwards a member of the Convention, nevertheless succeeded in carrying out the suggestion. Fouché, too, took part in the deputation, and with his companions had to submit to a mild reproof from the President of the Society, who reminded them of the dignified moderation of the Oratorian attitude in the past.

Fouché had, however, made his début in the character in which posterity will always remember him—that of the man who was continually making his appearance in a new and unexpected rôle. After this he was looked upon as one of the disturbing elements in the Order, and

35

was transferred from stormy Arras to Nantes, where a fairly conservative public feeling and his own civic ties might be expected to exercise a cooling influence upon the impulsive heat of his feelings. His reforming zeal was also doubtless somewhat quenched by the fact that the pupils in his school had begun to rebel against their teacher's "despotism". Fouché, who, in consequence of the increasing decay of the Oratorian Order, soon obtained the sole control of the school at Nantes, was fully occupied there in restoring discipline and tolerable work-conditions until May 1792, when this institution, in company with all others of the same character, was swept away by the blast of revolution.

But even temperate Nantes had its revolutionary club, *Les Amis de la Constitution*, a branch of that powerful, widespread society which was afterwards known as the *Jacobins*. Of this club Fouché became a member as early as November 1790, and he had scarcely been chosen as its President on February 17, 1791, before an incident occurred which revealed not only his inherent radical tendencies, but also the delicacy of his position in bourgeois Nantes and his talent for calm retreat when he had ventured on too bold an advance. He sent a note of congratulation to a member of the National Assembly, the well-known Brissot, on the occasion of a speech he had made for the abolition of slavery. But many of Fouché's fellow-citizens in Nantes owned negro plantations—as, for that matter, he did himself—so in a new address to Brissot he made a bold effort to explain away his words. But this in no way met with Brissot's approval, and he protested at seeing " a priest who calls himself a patriot appear as the champion of

36

the most revolting theft which is condemned by Holy Writ ", and exhorted Fouché not to write any more " at the dictation of dealers in human flesh and blood who bring discredit upon the philanthropy of your town ". Fouché was thus brought to the pillory ; for the first time, but not for the last, strong emphasis was laid on the contradiction between his radicalism and his place amongst the Oratorians. Brissot, indeed, had even stamped him as priest, a mistake, as we know, but, nevertheless, the origin of abuse levelled at Fouché all through his after-life. In this conflict, however, Fouché undoubtedly found himself on the safe side in sure alliance with those in power in his town, and this position was also one that was to become typical of his attitude in political life, i.e. in all subsequent conflicts. As Fouché's biographer, Madelin, expresses it, we have him already " whole and entire " in this interchange of opinions between him and Brissot.

Madelin also seems to vouch for the authenticity of another anecdote from the dawn of Fouché's political career which, moreover, is quite amusing. The universal effect of the Revolution in disturbing the mutual relations existing between officers and soldiers, public functionaries and subordinates, teachers and scholars, was also felt in the mercantile fleet of the good town of Nantes. The three-master *La Jeune Caroline* was at sea near Jamaica when the crew mutinied and threw the captain and pilot overboard. The vessel then drifted at the mercy of the wind until the crew chose as captain Boatswain Beaugenty, who, without more ado, instituted the most terrific discipline and brought the boat safe and sound into the harbour at Nantes. The crew were

37

greeted at first by the local revolutionary club with acclamation and the interchange of many a brotherly caress. Bitter complaints were uttered of the sailor's hard lot, and all were unanimous in criticizing the injustice of the officers, whom they wished to bring up before the legislative assemblies. Then Fouché mounted the rostrum amidst the attention that all were willing to give on this subject to the son of a respected sea-captain. With the objective outlook of an experienced schoolmaster, Fouché explained that he only wished to read a couple of documents that showed the significance of the tale of the three-master. They were two communications from one of the crew on the frigate *Atalanta,* and the first had been given at sea, on February 2, 1792. The crew had followed the example set on *La Jeune Caroline*: the first mate had been tossed overboard, the pilot hanged from the mainmast, and those of the officers who had shown any resistance were put in irons and shut up in the hold. Meantime a violent storm had blown up, and since none of the crew knew any navigation, although they all wished to be in command, the boat had simply been at the mercy of the winds. Fouché continued: " The disorder seemed but to add to the charm of the freedom which we had just achieved, and for its greater celebration and enjoyment the whole crew, who were beginning to get drunk, began to fight. Imagine the yells of the combatants, mingled with the revellers' songs and the roar of the waves and drowned in the peals of thunder. Under any other circumstances this scene would only have aroused our horror, but then it gave us pleasure, since it taught us to recognize the value of freedom."

In spite of all discomfort the crew yet had the satisfaction of seeing the rogue of a mate hanging from the yard-arm. " If we die, we die as free men. Long live liberty ! " Fouché is said to have enthusiastically repeated his concluding words, but only to be met by dead silence on every side. He passed on to the second communication from his alleged informant. After forty hours of mutiny and storm the frigate sank, and the survivors of the crew were left clinging to the rocks on which the *Atalanta* had been dashed. They managed to find refuge on a small island sheltered from the breakers. One of the shipwrecked mariners now, on his own initiative, assumed supreme command, with two others as assistants. They soon subdued their other comrades, who had to work fourteen hours a day on the land, to give up most of the harvest to their hard masters, and go hungry themselves, so that they began to regret their exploit.

When Fouché had finished, he told his audience he had only read from a newspaper. The effect was great, however ; embarrassed laughter was heard from the heroes of *La Jeune Caroline*, and the club dispersed without any resolution to bring the Nantes skippers to justice. The description has undoubtedly sufficient local colour to make it very credible, and Fouché, on this occasion, certainly had as great a personal reason to protect the interest of the seafaring citizens of Nantes as when he gave up the idea of the abolition of negro slavery. We need not, of course, assume that he had himself made up the moral tale that he related ; we, however, catch sight of him here too, " whole and entire ", preventing a crude and dangerous proceeding without using any stronger measures than the occasion required. With a masterly hand he applies his educational principles to a quite small political situation. In so doing he frames his course of action entirely on the turn of mind and opinions of those whom he is addressing, leads his hearers' imagination by degrees from the case under consideration on to a wider view of the matter, guides them to less prejudiced and calmer reflection concerning what they have in hand, mixes a touch of irony and satire in the apparent calm of his matter-of-fact narration, and irresistibly alters the trend of ideas and feelings. Even when he has only finished the first communication, Fouché's trumpet call of liberty falls flat and hollow upon the ears of those present, and, when the second has been delivered, there is an end as well to all outrageous, fantastic ideas of ruining the shipowners and captains in Nantes.

By his action on this occasion Fouché not only maintained and increased his authority in the revolutionary club, but also gained influential friends amongst the well-to-do citizens of his native town. In the same way, when the occasion arose later in Paris, he understood, in his capacity of Minister of the Police under Napoleon, how to keep on pleasant terms both with those who still remained revolutionaries and the returning *émigrés*.

Such were Fouché's political tactics in a nutshell. But difficult times were still to come before he got an opportunity to use them freely and successfully on a wider field, times of miscalculation and error that were ever after to affect adversely his political career and at last, in spite of all, to bring about his fall.

Is not this tale of the mutiny of the *Atalanta* told by Fouché in the spring of 1792, after all, but an epitome of the history of the whole French Revolution? It is the foreshadowing of the " bacchantes of Liberty ", to borrow Robespierre's expression, who had to atone for their excesses by slavery under a despot, of the regicides who became the dukes, counts and barons of the Emperor Napoleon's Court. It was, too, Fouché's own history that he, all unwittingly, told with his own lips to the Jacobins of Nantes.

Chapter IV

Fouché's Début in the Convention

A NEW stage of Fouché's life began in September 1792, when he married Bonne-Jeanne Coignaud, daughter of one of the higher administrative officials in his native town. There was no objection to be raised against this step, since he had never taken any vow of chastity. Mademoiselle Coignaud was then a young woman in the late twenties, " terribly ugly " and " red-headed, like her husband, even to eyebrows and lashes ", to quote from Vicomte Paul Barras, that practised specialist in questions of sex. But Fouché, who did not reach a high standard of beauty himself, gave her a true and loyal affection, and their marriage proved a happy one. Fouché was also elected, in September 1792, as a member of the National Convention, the Assembly that, after the destruction of the Monarchy in August, was to create new forms for the life of the French nation.

Public feeling in Nantes, even during this period of upheaval, was marked by great moderation. And this Fouché undoubtedly kept in view when making his election promises. These we might designate as a " popular programme ", intended to appeal to all in his demand for the election of a Breton by birth to look after the trade and shipping interests, in his promise of support in the maintenance of public order, and lastly by the assurance that he would continue those efforts in the direction of liberty which he had already begun

42

even as a teacher. There is, however, an unmistakably strong touch of democracy in these utterances of his ; for example, Fouché lays stress on the necessity of choosing men of character, adding that "by character is understood not so much remarkable genius as soundness of judgment, not so much brilliant talents as firm morals". Rather, in fact, a humdrum, practical moralist than an unworldly idealist ! In quite the style of any popular eighteenth-century philosopher, he states that he has "found that human sufferings exist in every period, but that political art consists in utilizing them for the general good, just as the moralist should use his knowledge to convert them into a benefit for the individual". At no distant date Fouché was to find that sufferings constitute a material more explosive and inflammable than any of the substances he had prepared during his teaching-years in the school laboratory.

Fouché, then, was to represent the department of Loire Inférieure in the National Convention. In common with his fellow-representatives there, he had to take an oath in which, amongst other things, he promised "to die for the safety of the individual and the sacred right of property". Under the conditions then existing, this meant that the deputies were to oppose any attempt of the Parisians to exercise arbitrary authority in the country. Fouché clearly understood the meaning of this part of his task, for he had scarcely become a member of the Convention when he wrote to his electors that "a handful of men shall no longer control the majority of the nation". Up to the very end of the year he managed to keep on a good footing with these employers of his, and in the latter part of

December he was elected to the Town Council of Nantes.

On September 21 the Convention met in the riding-school (*manège*) of the Tuileries Gardens in Paris; the seven hundred and forty-nine members were crowded together in groups of eager talkers on the seats arranged as in an amphitheatre. The only fact that stood out plainly amidst the prevailing feeling of hazy uncertainty was that France was now actually a republic, and that the future of the country lay completely in the hands of the Convention. When Fouché, all unnoticed, made his timid entrance into the assembly, he saw well-known faces in the seats to the left; and amongst them he caught a glimpse of Robespierre from Arras, with his spectacled, impassive face, surrounded by a circle of devoted admirers. Perhaps the sight awoke in the newly married Fouché embarrassed memories of Robespierre's sister, Charlotte; perhaps, too, his lips curled in an ironical smile at the sight of this morose fanatic who was for ever raising the cry of " To arms ! " throughout the Republic, somewhat as the geese had once cackled of impending ruin on the Roman Capitol. But the majority lay evidently on the right, in the Girondist group, and there, too, former friends awaited him, chief amongst them Daunou, fearless and lovable, once a leading light amongst the Oratorians both in literature and science. Fouché now gladly became intimate with Condorcet, the oracle of the Girondist party and permanent secretary of the French Academy of Science, as courteous and modest within the circle of his friends as he was dignified and reserved outside, " a volcano covered with snow ", the great theorist of

44

the Revolution, who certainly added even stronger conviction to Fouché's faith in the power and future of the enlightened ideas of the intellectuals. For the rest, the new arrival, Fouché, played a somewhat passive part in the Convention. He found his sphere of activity in the numerous committees that prepared the successful reforms in finance and legislation that were afterwards to prove a permanent result of the work of the Convention. He worked particularly on the education committee, where he espoused the cause of higher schools and showed his desire to bring them into line with the system developed by the Oratorian Order. He was also very anxious that the property which had been earmarked for the maintenance of the higher schools should continue to belong to them. It was a policy of moderation, well befitting a deputy from Nantes, and his work on the committees was good training for his after-career. In the frequent debates of a small private circle Fouché soon saw through the veil of phrases and principles that hid private inconsistencies, prejudices and passions, but he took good care not to cross-examine anyone for his opinions, rather avoiding, or respecting as far as possible, preserves where personal vanity stood on guard. He saw with concern the change that took place in opinions as expressed privately in committee or publicly in the Convention. The breeze, portending a storm, began to blow. The French ship of State had begun to drift after the fall of the Monarchy as *La Jeune Caroline* had done after the mutiny. If it was ever to come into port, a strong hand must take the helm. But were Fouché's friends the Girondists really suited for such a task ?

Chapter V

The Trial and Condemnation of Louis XVI

" THEY enter the Revolution garlanded with flowers, popular as soon as they are known. Palms go before them into the field of strife." Thus Edgar Quinet speaks of the men from the Gironde. The social work of the year 1789 had been in its essence their contribution to history, the assertion that precedence must bring with it responsibilities, the recognition of the equality of all in the eyes of the law, and the establishment of a class of peasant proprietors on small holdings. The burning enthusiasm of the Girondists for the external independence of France will also cast a glorious reflection for ever on these tragic figures. But with the advent of the Convention, politicians were faced with fresh tasks. It certainly might seem as if the Girondists ought still to have been called upon to guide and lead, to maintain the authority of the Convention against the encroachment of the Paris Commune, the right of the country against Paris, the policy of moderation against deeds of violence. And these duties, apparently so self-evident, were met, be it noticed, right up to the fall of the Girondists in June 1794 by acts of overwhelming force by the majority in the all-powerful Convention. In his essay on Barère, the Terrorist, Macaulay, in passing, severely criticizes the Girondists for their " criminal irresolution and want of sound judgment ". We find the explanation of this in the

46

fact that they were never a real political party under firm leadership, with discipline and a unanimous programme, but, instead, a coterie of talented individuals each acting on his own initiative. Their orators excelled themselves when listened to with bursts of applause, but were reduced to silence by organized ill-will. They never ceased to bring up the question of justice and forgot to show their power. Meantime the opposition to them increased. Their flashes of invective in debate were aimed without method at the vanity, first of one and then of another, and by degrees confirmed the view of the members of the Extreme Left that a virtuous and happy republic could only be built upon the ruins of the Girondist influence and reputation. But if the Girondist leaders did not rule their own party, they had still less influence with the people in the country. The Left, on the other hand, had a strong backing in the Paris Commune and the Jacobin Club, which by degrees was covering the whole of France with a network of branches.

It is evident that Fouché could not throw himself heart and soul into such a " party " as the Girondists.

After the overthrow of the Monarchy it was still necessary to determine the treatment to be meted out to the deposed King, " the thirty-third of Hugh Capet's line ". The Girondists detested Louis, that invertebrate weakling, who, to the very last, was in the hands of hypocritical priests and to whom the friendship of princes was of more importance than the sacred call of patriotism. But on the other hand—was it fitting for men to take revenge on such a creature ? The blade of the guillotine, falling on a defenceless victim at the

47

command of a wrangling national assembly, by no means reflected the brightness of the dagger raised by Brutus against an all-powerful tyrant. Is not pity for misery a sacred virtue, too, in the hearts of fellow-citizens? The Girondists wanted, however, to save the King, now rendered harmless, and at the same time to keep their personal reputation as republicans. In opposition to this half-hearted policy, the attitude of the Left was quite simple. Legal proceedings were unnecessary, for Louis could not be tried, since he had put himself outside the law. Or, to quote Robespierre's words on Louis's relations with foreign Powers, "Louis denounced his people as rebels, but the Revolution and the nation have shown that he is the only rebel." Thus the position was clear : for or against the Republic, life or death—there was no third alternative. In politics a strong will at last gains the victory over varying moods. Fouché could not help noticing how the influence of the Left, little by little, affected the majority in the Convention.

"The history of kings is the martyrdom of peoples ", was a favourite phrase with the Left. But something strange now happened. The martyr's halo was seen shining with sudden brightness round the head of the forsaken captive in the prison of Le Temple. Teaching his son, praying, meditating, enjoying the sleep of the just, he formed so striking a contrast to the picture of the cruel tyrant that he could not fail to appear the victim of unjust persecution. People were carried away by the warmth of their feelings, and baffled the suspicions of his guards by posing as his bitter enemies, simply to catch a glimpse of him, to get near him and,

LOUIS XVI

From a painting by Duménil

unperceived, to carry off some article that he had used or even touched. The history of the nation had been changed into the martyrdom of kings. Thus Louis in his humiliation became a greater danger for the Revolution than he had ever been before, in the days of his exaltation. But the party quarrel still continued in the Convention. The Girondists conquered so far that a trial was decided upon for Louis. But then general confusion and disorder ensued. The Girondists now wanted to follow up their victory by first declaring Louis " guilty of conspiring against the common safety of the State ", but then allowing a national vote to confirm or reject this judgment. By their first step they intended to pose as stern patriots, whilst by the second they vindicated the people's power with regard to their representatives. Their actual aim, however, was to concoct a plan by which Louis could be saved from the bloodthirsty Left, whilst the Girondists themselves were freed from all further personal responsibility. But meanwhile they endeavoured to hide their plan by the theatrical device of agreeing with the Left that the deputies should give their decision by open votes. The members of the Convention, in order of their departments, were one by one to mount the tribune and each record his vote aloud.

Thus on January 15, 1793, the Convention decided, by a practically unanimous vote, that Louis XVI was guilty of treachery against the nation. The first part of the Girondists' plan had been carried out successfully, but the very same day proved once more the truth of Jesus Sirach's saying that " cunning is not wisdom ", for the proposal to submit the decision to a public referendum was rejected by a majority of sixty-eight. On January 16th the Convention proceeded to decide on Louis's punishment. The Girondists were caught in their own trap. The public vote intended solely to prove their republican attitude had been but a test of their moral courage.

And where, we may ask, might Fouché be at this crisis? When the question was reached of the referendum to the nation, he voted with the Left, for the first time on any decision of importance. But so did many other members who, at the third question, endeavoured to save Louis from the death penalty. Fouché apparently had for some time belonged to these, for on January 15 he remarked to his friend Daunou that no doubt he would be surprised at the boldness he showed in opposing those who desired Louis's death. Indeed, on that same afternoon he handed to Daunou—a peerless stylist—the rough draft of his proposed speech, begging him to look it over critically, and also during the course of the voting to take his place in the middle of the Convention hall and by signs regulate Fouché's tones. His rough draft contained a rejection of the death sentence.

The time of voting drew near. Fouché's former colleague at the Juilly school in Paris, now a radical member of the Left, Billaud-Varennes—a very conspicuous figure in his red wig—hastened all day long from seat to seat, spreading the news that the majority were already won for Louis's death sentence. Members made calculations and argued, whilst many were drawn as by a magnet over to what they imagined would be the winning side. But it was not before eight o'clock in the evening that the fatal point in the agenda was reached.

After that, the hours of the cold winter night passed slowly enough. Flickering lamps and candles lit up no more than half of the long rectangular hall, with its two low galleries. Members came and went feverishly through the doors, eagerly debating their various intrigues, whilst the air grew more and more oppressive and heavy. But anyone glancing at the seats, reserved in the gallery above the Left benches, might have fancied himself spirited away to a State evening at the opera. Elegant ladies in evening dress, adorned with bright tricolour ribbons, were there, enjoying ices and oranges. Higher up, the gallery was free to the public, who were constantly on the move, as they kept their spirits up to concert pitch with wine and brandy. Down in the body of the hall, meantime, there was nothing but weary impatience and suspense. Now and again a member was overcome by sleep, and had to be suddenly wakened when it was his turn to vote. As the long procession of pale faces, even paler in the poor light, passed by the tribune, the silence was only broken by the ever-recurring echo of two slow, sad words : *La mort, la mort !* This test split the ranks of the Girondists. Their foremost member, Vergniaud, President of the Convention on that day, unexpectedly went over to the enemy's camp, but more merciful judgments were pronounced as well. The tension grew ; a dull uneasiness took possession of the weary ranks of the Convention.

Then came the turn of the department Loire Inférieure, Fouché's immediate circle. Daunou was in his place to help his friend. Varying opinions were uttered by Fouché's comrades, some demanding that Louis should be kept in captivity during the war and exiled at its conclusion, others that he should be expelled from the country at once. One spoke for his death, another objected to it. Then Fouché's face suddenly appeared on the tribune, white as death, impassive and inscrutable as ever. Daunou listened, but only one utterance was heard from the orator's pale lips : *La mort !* Then he was gone, and a fresh figure appeared upon the platform.

The hours passed by. The first streak of dawn came and grew until it was full daylight once more ; the lights were put out, but still the ghostly procession of speakers passed on through the hall. Nor was there any thinning of its ranks until towards evening. But at 8 p.m. all was finished, and Vergniaud, in trembling tones, announced the result. By a majority of one Louis had been condemned to death. It was eleven at night before the Convention brought this historic meeting to a close. Michelet tells us that a general illumination was ordered in the name of public safety. But nothing could have been more depressing than lights from every window falling upon deserted streets, an attempt at rejoicing that ended in failure and only produced a sense of sadness. All night the newsvendors ran through the streets crying : *La mort, la mort !*

The tragedy went on to its end. The demand for a respite, with which a number of the members sought to veil their doubts, was rejected by the Left under the unctuous pretext that the interests of humanity demanded that the prisoner should not have to endure any further torture of uncertainty. On January 21, 1793, Louis met his death to the roll of muffled drums. It is said that even his executioners dipped their weapons and garments in his blood to keep them as relics.

Chapter VI

Terrorist

Fouché had settled his account with the past. His behaviour reached a still lower level from the fact that he pretended to Daunou that he had voted under pressure of threats from revolutionaries in Nantes and in compliance with his wife's entreaties. Besides, of how little weight was *his* vote! A justifiable attempt has been made to find a very different explanation. Fouché no longer had any faith in the future of the Girondist Party. In the eyes of Robespierre's followers, the fact that he came from bourgeois Nantes and his association with the party of the Right were so many reasons to distrust him. Fouché had a faint inkling that here was a chance to clear himself in a moment and took means to follow it. The shadow of Louis XVI's scaffold would fall for ever upon his life, for, by his vote, he had shared in the resolution that had fixed a gulf between republican France and Old Europe, and transformed their mutual dissensions into a fight for principles. The breach between them was now past healing, but, as Sorel has emphatically pointed out, this hostility made it necessary for France to arm herself against accumulated dangers, and hence, in due season, arose her military power. Thus the Napoleonic era already loomed ahead during those January days of 1793 in the crowded hall of the Convention.

Fouché, for his part, was not like his celebrated

fellow-member Siéyès, content to "live" through the hard time of the Reign of Terror, and that fatal January 16, 1793, marks a fresh stage in his career. It is true that later on he made an effort to get back to his original position, and he seemed once again to have assumed his former attitude, but the step had been too decisive to be retraced. That is why we have always to return to his shattered and harassed existence during 1793 and 1794 to discover the secret that followed him, like a ghost, through all his remaining years, and continually made its presence felt in spite of his vain efforts at exorcism by attempting to persuade himself and others that his actions had always been the result of inevitable necessity.

Fouché's transformation after January 16, 1793, appears, to begin with, as a change of opinion. When President of the Jacobin Club in Nantes in 1792, he had dubbed as weak the ruler who is "cruel and kills to-day the enemy that he may have to fear to-morrow". Generosity was for him, then, the distinctive sign of a wise policy, for in the autumn of the same year, in a letter to Condorcet, he recommends a conciliatory attitude even towards the Royalist priests, in spite of their shifty and underhand nature and of their overbearing habit of intermeddling. He says : " I believe that real indulgence, limited confidence and strict but secret supervision would chain and muzzle the monster whose pride is roused by a haughty and irritable rule, and who, accustomed to conquer by deceptive lures, can only be conquered by the same method." There is no doubt that this conciliatory method is Fouché's sincere recommendation, and bears the personal stamp of his calm and ironical deliberation. But it is quite another tale after that January resolution. He at once puts before the public exhaustive reasons for his vote, and then pours contempt on timid creatures who " shrink back at the shadow of a King", speaks of the indignation that fills his heart at " the tyrant's crime ", and says that if he was not quickly struck by the sword of justice, " robbers and murderers might go their way in open defiance ". There is evidently no longer any question of proving his strength by gentleness or of the best possible manipulation of human passions and vices. For or against ! There is no middle course.

Such words from a man who but lately had meant to oppose Louis's death sentence cannot be looked upon as an impulsive temperamental outburst, but must rather be a considered utterance. This view is also supported by Fouché's future attitude. Whilst the republican reign of virtue takes shape but slowly during the course of 1793, Fouché in the early part of the year proclaims an independent vindication of all the fundamental principles of republicanism. His electors in Nantes were surprised as early as the beginning of February by a manifesto from Fouché to the local Jacobin Club in which he makes a violent attack on the egoists of the Right for their want of strength and enthusiasm, and in which, too, he, the well-to-do citizen's son from Pellerin, draws a cynical comparison between the " high and mighty bourgeois " and " the useful worker ". Fouché had plainly not only taken the side of radical Paris against rural conservatism, but also gone over to the idea of a social, possibly an economic, revolution as the sequel to the political upheaval. In the Convention, Fouché, during March, brought about a law to prevent *émigrés*—who at this time had been sent into perpetual exile—from privately selling their property in France. " The man who avenges himself other than by the power of the law is ", he declares, " a murderer, and those who, for private revenge, draw the sword of war against their fatherland are parricides." But such a crime is, above all, theirs who appeal to foreign help against their own country. Thus the *émigrés* fell under the crushing sentence expressed in the poet's words :—

> He who betrays his land has neither
> Family, nor race, nor son, nor father.

According to this view, of course, France and those who chanced to be in power were one and the same thing.

The French Republic of the regicides had, however, still one bitter enemy, a heritage from the Girondists' struggle with monarchy—the royalty priesthood, who, through the length and breadth of the land, had snared the nation in a net whose meshes were all the stronger because invisible. Consequently Fouché looked round for a fatal weapon to use in his conflict with the priests, and found it on the field of popular education. This must be made not only compulsory and universal, but, above all, it must be entirely in the hands of the revolutionary Government, and all private educational institutions must be swept away. Such was the conclusion that Fouché, who so lately had been trying to maintain the Oratorian schools, now put forward without the slightest hesitation. " The schools of superstition and

prejudice must be destroyed." Their aim must be
" to lay the foundations of the eternal power of reason ".
Unity must be achieved in the nation's guiding principles,
and its foundation must be already laid in the child's
impressionable mind. " For ", says Fouché, in those
Thoughts concerning Public Education which he published
in June 1793, " otherwise frightful cleavage will result
from the influence of dissentient teachers." " The
one speaks in the name of God, whose interpreter and
servant he says he is ", and characterizes his religion
and its moral laws " as the only means that can open
the gates of heaven. He wishes to turn man into an
automaton, in whom custom and obedience take the
place of reason. The other, who knows the language
of truth and who wishes to make a man of his pupil,
only speaks to him of religions in order to remove the
veil that hides their origin. He teaches him the knowledge of his rights and duties as well as the rules he must
obey to achieve the happiness of himself and others in
this world, not in the next."

These " Thoughts " are worthy of note, since they
present Fouché under quite another aspect, i.e. as a
pioneer taking up arms for his faith and convictions.
The democratized Church which the Revolution had set
up in July 1790 has been justly characterized as a popular
State Church that retained its former Catholic character.
In spite of religious dissensions, persecutions and disputes, public opinion in 1793 was still influenced by
respect for the old-established customs of the Church.
If any occasional attacks did take place, they were
generally—so Aulard, the French historian of the
Revolution, states—the result of patriotic indignation

against the priests, who were at the beck and call of the King or of foreign Powers, and up to June 1793 there had not been any marked instances of even such indignation. But Fouché's utterances, given above, are of a plainly atheistic nature, since they point to life in this world rather than to a future existence as the goal of our efforts, and proclaim the " manly " doctrine that a citizen should devote his strength exclusively to obligations more advantageous to the community at large. It was the atheistic tendency in the intellectual movement of the eighteenth century which appeared without disguise in these speeches of Fouché's.

Now, is this change in Fouché real or only apparent? Is this the chameleon who changes his colour with his surroundings, or the convert speaking in the faltering accents of his newly-inspired tongue? There can scarcely be a doubt as to the answer to these questions. Fouché was, without any scruples, taking up a decided party attitude. How was this? The extraordinary nature of the time had taken entire possession of his impressionable temperament. The memory of the crime, the irrevocable murder of the King, came back again and again. And then the elementary sense of self-preservation made its voice heard. It was as strong as the sense of danger, and therefore strongest of all in the man whose anxiety, foresight and sense of reality were the most pronounced. No wonder then if Fouché became one of the worst extremists. In such a situation he had no difficulty in finding arguments for his radical attitude. He only needed to carry to a logical conclusion the thoughts that once had flashed across his mind in his laboratory and which he had discussed with such as Condorcet. But nature will recur even though expelled with a fork, as the classics have it. The terrorist helmet presses more and more heavily on Fouché's slight shoulders, until at last he seizes an opportunity to lift it up. But its iron has scarred him for ever. Error has bred fresh error, guilt is heaped upon guilt. Such is the history of Representative Fouché, a history which, at the same time, reflects a portentous chapter in the destiny of France.

Chapter VII

Iconoclast

IT was in 1793 that the enormous general levy of troops took place. The well-to-do were forced to part with their means to provide the soldiers' equipment, the requisite number of fighters were drawn by lot, and the forces supplemented later by an appeal to the communes, who, in their turn, showed a predilection for calling up those in better positions to military service. The conciliatory phrases of the public proclamations give us a picturesque description of the way in which the democratic national army is to be formed : " The young men go to battle, the married men forge the weapons and convey the necessaries of life. The women make tents and clothing and help in the hospitals. The children prepare lint, whilst the old men are carried to public places to incite the fighters' courage and their hatred against kings."

It was this feeling of exaltation, deeply tinged with glowing patriotism, that surrounded Fouché and carried him farther and farther into the stream. In March 1793, then, the Reign of Terror began. The Convention instituted a new instrument of government, the Committee of Public Welfare, whose members were only to hold office for a month, when fresh elections took place. A revolutionary Tribunal, which, in common with similar tribunals in the provinces, was to put in practice a new law against the enemies of the Revolution, was established in Paris. Leaders and led alike suffered the death penalty. All these measures were carried by the vote of a frightened Girondist majority, but in the night of May 31–June 1 the Left gained the complete upperhand in the Convention. The Girondist leaders were got rid of by clever co-operation on the part of the Convention minority and the Paris Commune. Cannon were brought up to the Convention doors and made all resistance impossible.

After this the character of the Convention changed, and its chief business was to record the resolutions passed by the Committee of Public Welfare, working at this time with feverish zeal. The centres of power were now—with the exception of the Paris Commune —the Jacobin Clubs, that, by means of their various branches, extended their control over the whole country. Every commune was ruled by its revolutionary club and its elected Revolution committee, but the Convention Representatives on Mission kept an eye on everything, and each, like an absolute monarch in his own district, made laws, set up tribunals, arrested, condemned to death, collected taxes, fixed wages and prices, received personal accusations, in addition to weeding out and transforming the leading circles of the communes. The mass of the nation held aloof in anxious silence from all this convulsive and arbitrary rule, carried on by a few men who, over and above all else, kept a jealous watch on one another's sins of omission and commission.

The sombre background for this desperate policy was a universal rise in prices and scarcity of corn, an urgent danger from without that became more acute in April after the French General Dumouriez had gone over to the enemy, and also—last but not least—a wave of rebellion that spread over Normandy and Brittany, south of the Loire into la Vendée, over several places in the north-east, and out towards the Rhone Valley. There was reason to fear that the civil war, kindled by the Royalists and Girondists, might unite with the attack of foreign enemies into a common conflagration that would not only entirely destroy the young Republic, but also the idealistic gain of liberty and fraternity.

*　　*　　*　　*　　*

In March 1793 Fouché, now a deputy of some standing in the Convention, was sent as Representative to la Vendée, where the flames of the Royalist insurrection were burning most fiercely. The peasant smallholders there were embittered against the Revolution, which had driven their priests into exile, and they were now roused to desperation by the conscriptions *en masse*. What concern of theirs were the enemies on the Eastern frontier? The real enemy was to be found in Paris! The Convention were still under wretched leadership, their headquarters like gipsy encampments, with " play-actors turned into generals, with their jugglers and conjurers accompanied everywhere by the most repulsive of girls ", according to the testimony of an eye-witness. In May, Nantes was the only fortified place in the neighbourhood of the rebellion which still remained unshaken by it. Under such conditions Fouché achieved no remarkable success. He increased his bad odour in his native place by demanding an increasing tax from the well-to-do, but failed in his attempt to recruit a new corps from the local officials. He also suppressed his own old Jacobin Club, which had failed to keep pace with his rapid turn to the Left. At last he seized the first favourable opportunity of returning to Paris. It was not until June that the efforts to put down the rebellion were successful, at any rate temporarily.

At the end of June Fouché was sent on a mission of a less active nature, viz. to recruit soldiers at Troyes in Champagne, against la Vendée, a work which he performed with no less tact than success. In Lyons, meantime, open and violent rebellion had arisen as a protest against the forcible overthrow of the Girondists. Fouché was near this district, since he now took up his abode in Nevers, on the Loire. Even here he found the population rebellious and ill-disposed. The local manufacturers, landowners and heads of glass-factories detested the Revolution that incited the lower classes and workers against them, thus causing them trouble in their various industries. Fouché meantime began gently, but on August 14 he set on foot a demonstration of a curious nature, in which his lower-middle class instincts as father of a family were found in almost touching union with an audacious craving for innovation. His good wife, Jeanne, who had loyally accompanied him on his mission as the apostle of freedom, gave birth to a daughter, an occasion of happy excitement amongst all the faithful in Nevers. Military and civil officials waited upon the happy parents at the head of the local National Guard, discoursing the loud strains of Janissary music. With the baby at its head, the whole procession marched to the market-place,

64

where the National altar had been set up. With sacerdotal solemnity Fouché proclaimed the birth of his daughter, chose sponsors from the company of well-wishers, and named her Nièvre, after her birthplace. The performance was not without a touch of unsophisticated carnival festivity, but the whole ceremony struck a blow at the good old faith and customs, and introduced similar proceedings in different parts of the country.

Clouds now began to gather over the path of Revolution. Anxiety gave rise to fanaticism, which became more and more violent as time went on. Enemies must be annihilated, their fastnesses destroyed, their idols overthrown and burnt. Otherwise all was lost! But an enemy was found in everyone who lacked the right republican and democratic turn of mind. It was such sentiments as these that drove Fouché ever farther on his path. Soon, too, he got a secret ally as a fellow Representative in Chaumette, the Paris terrorist, who took delight in appealing to the cruel sufferings of the poor to incite them against those of their fellow-countrymen who were more favourably placed. Thus, at the end of August 1793, a new and harder rule began in Nevers and its vicinity, and soon spread southward to Moulins in the direction of rebellious Lyons. On September 29 Chaumette was able to write to Paris that Fouché had done more good than he himself had achieved in all his life.

In Nevers Fouché issued an edict by which he became the forerunner of the iconoclasts, that were soon to put an end to the Catholic Church throughout the whole of France. No religious emblem, cross or image of any saint was to be allowed in any public place; no sacerdotal garb was to be worn in the streets. Ostensibly this was to put all religious denominations on an equal footing; atheism, however, peeps out in the regulation that adherents of various creeds were to bury their dead in a common burial-ground, that was to have no other adornment than trees and a statue representing sleep, whilst the inscription over the gate was to be: "Death is an eternal sleep." This was an attempt at a radical destruction of the influence exercised by the priests, for it was a denial of a life to come which was their promised reward to the faithful and their threat of punishment to backsliders. In this way Fouché endeavoured to put into practice the teachings he had set forth in his pamphlet on national education. Moreover, he compelled the local priests either to marry within a month or to adopt children.

Not even the church-buildings themselves were safe from the intrusion of Fouché's revolutionary fanaticism. As early as September 22, Fouché commandeered the church of St. Cyr in Nevers for a revolutionary festival. A bust of Brutus, who slew Cæsar, his dearest friend, with a dagger drawn in defence of republican principles, was placed on the altar and invoked by Fouché and Chaumette at the head of the local authorities and members of the Jacobin Club, escorted by a band of music. The festival ended with a meal for old people, who were waited upon by the two formidable National Representatives. Four days afterwards, things were even worse in Moulins. After Fouché had given utterance in the pulpit of the local church of Notre Dame to purely communistic doctrines, he marched at

66

the head of a procession through the town, allowing crosses, pictures and relics to be either destroyed or confiscated. All the copes and chasubles they could find were gathered together and made into a bonfire, round which they danced like savages. The bishop of the city, with a following of thirty priests, solemnly abjured their office.

The pillaging of churches and castles was hastily continued in the neighbouring district, and harvests poured in to the Convention Representatives. As early as September 11, Fouché sent off 100,000 gold marks[1] to the Convention, on October 18, 1,200 pounds of bar gold and 1,081 marks of ten ounces silver, and on October 29 seventeen packing-cases of chalices and chasubles. This last-named dispatch also included a gilt ducal crown, perhaps an omen of Fouché's own future. It was immediately smashed to pieces by a hot-blooded member of the assembly. Fouché accompanied his brilliant gifts by outpourings against the harm wrought by the precious metals to the Republic. Veritable baits as they were for covetous greed, they had done more harm to the public than the sword of their enemies. The existence of the metals, too, decreased the popularity of the paper money and assignats issued by the Republic. He ended by ascribing a mystic significance to his gold and silver: " Let us trample these idols of the Monarchy in the dust beneath our feet if we wish to secure adoration for the gods of the Republic and to establish the worship of liberty's stern virtues." The only things desired by a true republican are the Spartan riches of " bread and

[1] A mark = ½ lb.

iron ". The Convention was loud in Fouché's praises, but Robespierre, that incorruptible guardian of public morals, wrinkled his brows. What pickings had that quiz of a Fouché got from all this extortion? It is true that Fouché does not appear to have amassed any private wealth in his official appointment, but he and his friends certainly chose sumptuous fare with which to fortify themselves for their arduous task. Enormous bills bear witness to the consumption of southern wines, capons, pike, and all kinds of delicacies at the Representatives' table, of the unstinted purchase of clothes, frills, shirts and ruffles. It was a new upper-class of *nouveaux-riches* who held their court with open doors.

Within a short time Fouché became the central figure of a swarm of Revolution Committees in the surrounding district. These were authorized by him to institute domiciliary examinations, to sequestrate property in the owners' absence, to make inventories and confiscations, all with the help of a newly-formed flying " revolutionary army " of two hundred and fifty men. For the social revolution kept pace with the religious. The Convention had given the signal for war on this front as early as May, when it had fixed the minimum rate of wages and the maximum price of goods, and had made the producers responsible for the supply of foodstuffs, besides taking a forced loan from the wealthy of a milliard francs. Fouché's economic programme in Nevers and Moulins was, moreover, quite simple, namely, to take from the superfluity of the well-to-do and to give to the poor; indeed, he instituted by means of the Revolution Committees a systematic persecution of all who had comfortable means, since he saw in their prosperity another line of defence for the aristocracy and the opponents of the democratic Republic. If anyone let portions of his land lie fallow, these were at the mercy of the first person who wished to use them. Anyone who suspended work in his factory was punished under suspicion of plotting against the public. Capital was heavily taxed. The reason given for the spoliation was public charity, the relief of the aged, fatherless, destitute and poor. It was a brutal beginning to the measure that the Convention was to carry through in May 1794, for placing the public care of the poor on a democratic basis. But Fouché cannot be called a Socialist. His aim was limited to a fairer division of property, and he scarcely thought of allowing the State to take over the nation's supplies and means of production.

The undermining of the Church's position which Fouché had begun was meantime having a far-reaching effect, and his October decree to take away the Christian character of burial-grounds was copied both in Auvergne and Gascony. Throughout France, indeed, anger was brewing against the priests, those secret allies of the foreign foe. In October 1793 the Convention instituted the revolutionary calendar, which, with its three monthly holidays (*décadis*), was intended to suppress many Church customs connected with the old-established division into weeks. Churches were shut here and there with offensive processions, and priests unctuously abjured their office on the altars of their native land. Extremists in the Paris Convention

69

hastened under these conditions to follow up Fouché's lead, which was trumpeted abroad by Chaumette. Notre Dame was converted in somewhat operatic fashion into a temple of Reason, and a pretty actress, Mademoiselle Aubry, who represented the Goddess of Reason, was borne by willing arms to the Convention, where she received a fraternal kiss from the President of the assembly. The Convention confirmed the action of the Paris Commune, but in addition confined itself to a decision that every commune was free to act as it thought fit in its relations to the Church. Later on, in the autumn, Robespierre succeeded in stemming the anti-religious movement.

Chapter VIII

Lyons

LYONS, in spite of its defence by the united forces of Royalists and Girondists, had fallen into the hands of the Republic on October 9, 1793. A couple of days later, Couthon, second in authority to Robespierre in the Committee of Public Welfare, made his entry into the unfortunate city. In accordance with the latest humanitarian principle that the punishment of a single leading conspirator did more for freedom's cause than that of a hundred of those he had misled, Couthon showed a certain discrimination in his use of the guillotine. But two hundred victims did not satisfy Chaumette and his mad following in the Convention, and it was determined to make an example by entirely destroying Lyons, that insolent and rebellious town, by mines and fire, and afterwards naming the scene of desolation the *Commune Affranchie*, the Liberated Commune. The result of this resolution is seen in the fact that the population of Lyons was reduced by flight and persecution from 140,000 to about 80,000 souls.

The Convention now provided Fouché with a colleague and instrument for his work of slaughter in Collot d'Herbois, who had proposed in the Convention the utter destruction of Lyons. This Collot had, in earlier days, been one of a touring theatrical company, and his chief merit as an actor is said to have been displays of sentiment which at last became so realistic that

71

they quite overcame even the actor himself; report also states that he thoroughly appreciated the supper when the performance was ended! Nor was he changed as a terrorist. The sentimental feeling of an artistic temperament for human suffering and impatience of criticism drove him to join the extreme Left as a bitter opponent of any sign of moderation. Yet, in his way, Collot was one who, when occasion required, could take up the cudgels for his actions. Fouché probably did not get on so well as executioner in Lyons as with his apostolic work in Nevers. At any rate he sheltered behind Collot d'Herbois, who liked being spokesman, and, besides, occupied an important position as a member of the Committee of Public Welfare.

Lyons, with its 50,000 industrial workers, was, at the outbreak of the Revolution, undoubtedly a centre of social want and misery, and its poverty was increased by the general upheaval and the periodical financial crises. It was in Lyons that, later on, Charles Fourrier delivered his teachings as a standard-bearer of Socialism, and it was also the home of Marie-Joseph Chalier, who, like Fourrier, was a trader coming into personal touch with the discontented masses of workers. But Chalier lacked Fourrier's systematic methods, and, Italian as he was by birth, he reminds us rather, in the midst of his anarchistic fury, of the founder of some mediæval order. Little and delicate, with a yellow skin, flashing eyes and thick lips, he became the eloquent spokesman of the slums, " his heart ", to quote Michelet's expression, " sick with sympathy ". He was an enthusiastic supporter of the Revolution, and on his frequent visits to Paris brought home stones from the fallen Bastille, which he distributed as relics amongst the poor; but he was also given to outbursts of fury, not only against the nobility, the clergy and the rich, but against all who were above the average, such as officials, lawyers or artists. In February 1793 there arose a wild and possibly groundless report that Chalier, who had been chosen as Mayor of the town, intended to form a revolutionary tribunal and institute a general massacre of his opponents. When, in May, Lyons rose against the Terror, Chalier and his followers were thrown into prison. He, who had seen in Christ only the god of the rich, "the tyrant of souls", soared to religious heights in his farewell to his friends. "I embrace all who remember me, I love you, I love them, just as I love all mankind. Farewell. I go to rest in the bosom of the Eternal." But he assured the Court that condemned him that his death would cost his executioners dear. His death was horrible. The guillotine was worn out, and the blade had to fall three times before its work was done.

Fouché's and Collot's joint work in Lyons was introduced on November 10 by a memorial feast in honour of Chalier; all Lyons was to be offered as a gigantic sacrifice to this spirit, thirsting for revenge. The festival began, of course, with iconoclasm. Fouché and Collot swept through the streets from church to church at the head of a company of workmen, each carrying either a hatchet or an axe. Next they bore a bust of Chalier with a memorial urn in solemn procession through Lyons, whilst the mob yelled out their "Down with the aristocrats!" "Long live the guillotine!" In the procession a donkey was led, dressed

73

up in carnival fashion in cope and mitre with a crucifix, a Bible and the Gospels fastened to his tail. The procession stopped at the Place des Terreaux, and the Convention Representatives fell prostrate in the dust before Chalier's bust. They then made speeches, and Fouché declared : " The blood of the guilty is the only atoning stream that can constrain your justly enraged spirit to rest." A small bonfire was made of the Bible and Gospels, whilst the donkey was offered water in a chalice. Then sudden heavy rain put an end at once to all the vulgar proceedings. A bust of Chalier's was now put up in all the churches and a republican and civic cult introduced. His death-mask was sent to the Convention, where members shuddered at the sight of his wounds. Then followed the systematic work of destruction. Fouché and Collot worked feverishly in their office, where entrance was granted to none but the revolutionary officials and members of the Jacobin Club, and only to these on a written application stating the nature of their business. A revolutionary Tribunal was instituted and called from its President the *Comité Parein*. Its starting-point was the legislation with reference to " suspects " which the Convention had made in August and September, and which ordained that all were to come under this heading who by behaviour, private connections, words or writings had shown themselves opposed to liberty, and that all " suspects " were to be imprisoned. How many then were imprisoned in a conquered, rebellious town like Lyons ! With no more ado, all were looked upon as guilty of plotting against the Government. That meant a speedy expedition before the terrifying judges,

74

who were arrayed in three-cornered hats with the tri-
coloured cockade, and wore round their necks ribbons
of the same colour to which a little axe was attached.
On one occasion forty accused prisoners were sentenced
in half an hour by a mere sign on the part of the judges,
and all of them to death !

On December 12 the executions began on the Brotteaux Place, in the city of Lyons. A platform was
erected where the Convention Representatives sat,
Fouché, so tradition says, calmly viewing the distressing
spectacle through his lorgnette. Two trench-graves
had been dug side by side, and between them were
ranged the sixty-four condemned to die, all young
persons, fastened together in couples. The cannon
were placed to cover these fatal rows. The silence
was broken, strangely enough, by the voices of the
victims singing a farewell hymn. The Representatives
gave the signal, and the cannon-balls pierced their way
through their great target. The song was changed
into cries of pain. The soldiers' sabres at last gave the
death-stroke to every one. And yet, according to
Collot d'Herbois, this agitating scene was but a general
rehearsal, and, time after time, the horrible proceeding
was repeated. An order was given to throw the lifeless
bodies into the Rhone, that they might drift down the
river and strike terror into the rebels of Toulon. When
the *Comité Parein* was dissolved again on April 5, 1794,
it had put to death, generally with the harquebus,
but also with the guillotine as well, 1,667 persons of
different ages. The plaintive cry from Lyons soon
penetrated even to Paris, and Collot made a journey
thither at the end of December to try to justify himself

and his colleagues. In the Jacobin Club he even attempted to cover their misdeeds with the garment of mercy : " We have had two hundred shot at once, and you lay that to our charge as a crime. Do you not know that is rather a sign of commiseration? When twenty criminals are guillotined, the last to be executed has already died twenty times, whilst the two hundred conspirators die but once." He did but disclose the extent of his depravity by endeavouring, with such cold-blooded sentimentality, to sound the depths of the lacerated feelings of those condemned to die.

The destruction of Lyons palace and the systematic robbery of the local bourgeois citizens went on side by side with the executions. Coats, breeches, shoes— everything was commandeered from them under pretext of the needs of the army or of the poor. It was like being under foreign rule in an enemy's land. The champions of liberty proceeded against their adversaries with the same mad fury as, in former times, the soldiers of the Reformation displayed in Rome of the Renaissance.

" A bayonet piercing a human breast makes me tremble, but this bayonet is guiltless, and only a child would wish to break it "—this was the picture that Fouché drew, a year later, of his share in the devastation at Lyons. " Extenuating circumstances " are indeed not entirely absent as a defence of his course of action. The orders of the Convention and the presence of the terrible Collot gave the keynote there. In a word, at the end of the eighteenth century executions belonged everywhere to the order of the day, even in peaceful times. Notwithstanding this, Fouché had a private warning given to threatened persons ; indeed, he even advised priests to keep out of the way. He fetched from Paris more moderate Jacobins whom he distributed amongst the Revolution Committees to work against Chalier's revengeful friends. When, in January 1794, Collot d'Herbois was absent from Lyons and Fouché began to think that a more reconciliatory attitude under the powerful leadership of Danton was likely to win the day in Paris, he at once changed his tactics. On February 2 he ordered the harquebusshooting to stop and a return to the more accurate aim of the guillotine. In the middle of the month he issued an order that all penalties for the rebellion should cease entirely. In the middle of March the greater number of the Revolution Committees working in and round Lyons were dissolved. Fouché plainly stigmatized them as " a political canker ". It is strange that a politician of such keen insight as Fouché should have been so utterly mistaken as to the situation in Paris, where Robespierre's authority was becoming more and more pronounced, whilst, at the same time, he was showing a growing tendency to adopt plainly terrorist principles. In conclusion we may say that Fouché showed this moderation, although he had believed in all good faith that a rebellion such as that in Lyons must be remorselessly suppressed if the work of the Revolution was to be maintained.

Is this enough to clear his memory of a blood-stained record? For his contemporaries it was not enough, nor can posterity be content to look upon him as a weak-willed creature, who had to lend himself to a little of everything. Collot d'Herbois, who never shirked his responsibility, but expiated it with his death

77

in the swamps of Guiana, finds with us—and with justice —greater favour than Fouché, who afterwards hid away just as a fox crouches down in the ploughed field until the worst of the danger is past. But Fouché's name is still found to-day under the fatal resolutions, and he had assisted at the institution of the entire revolutionary apparatus which, without distinction, ground all to powder that offended Jacobin self-assurance. Meantime it is a conclusive fact that the inquisitorial inquiry in Lyons was still in force long after the foreign foes had been driven back and the internal revolution subdued. Or, as G. Pariset, the latest historian on the French Revolution, expresses it : " The coercion was severe only in Lyons, and since it grew but slowly to excess, it is permissible to draw the conclusion that it was not unavoidable."

Chapter IX

Robespierre and Fouché

In the beginning of April 1794 Fouché was suddenly recalled to Paris. The contest between Robespierre and his opponents both on the Right and Left was already at an end. On April 5 Danton, condemned to death for treachery to the Republic, had mounted the scaffold on the Place de la Concorde, the last of a long line of companions in misfortune. His gigantic silhouette stood out, as the Parisian writer, Georges Cain, tells us in his picturesque way, against the purple of the evening sky. Amidst the darkening shadows, the unquenchable revolutionary seemed to be rising from his grave rather than awaiting the stroke from the guillotine that was to end his life, and an overpowering shudder of gloom passed through the trembling crowd. Even the extremists of the Paris Commune had been crushed by Robespierre. Fouché's colleague in Nevers, Chaumette, was in prison awaiting his last hour, and when Fouché himself crept into the Convention hall, he discovered everywhere amongst the seats the vacant places of friends who had been struck down by party revenge. Their followers wandered round without a leader. Sixty members of the Convention no longer dared to live in their homes for fear of an order to arrest them. Yet the feeling of terror did but increase Fouché's power of resistance. He asked permission to speak at once to justify to the

Convention his course of action in Lyons. In vain! He was not allowed to say a word, and amidst ill-omened silence his report was sent for scrutiny to the Committee of Public Welfare. He had reason to fear the worst from the triumvirate now ruling the Committee, viz. Couthon, who had had to yield to him in Lyons; Saint-Just, the terrorist with the heart of a fanatic and the self-satisfied face of a pretty child, the man who, as the whisper went, " carried his head as if it were the Holy Sacrament " ; and Robespierre himself.

To withdraw from his position would have simply been to await with outstretched hands his *coup de grâce*, and the first essential for victory was rather to come to an understanding as soon as possible with the enemy. So that very evening Fouché hastened to Robespierre, the ruler of the State, who lived in democratic simplicity in the house of citizen Dupleix, a carpenter and joiner of Rue St. Honoré, No. 398. He was admitted in the usual order to the presence of " the Incorruptible ", delicate and thin, scraggy even, but who, dressed in the customary immaculate frills and pale blue frock-coat, appeared more remote and haughty than ever, whilst a dark shadow fell over Fouché's death's-head physiognomy, with the clear-cut nose and projecting cheek-bones. The silence seemed to tell its own tale. So Fouché the robber, the atheist, was there, destroyed by his own guilt! There was no question of clemency; justice must have its way with the robber of sacred buildings just as with the tyrants' slaves. Robespierre, as always, acted in accordance with his principles. Waving aside Fouché's outstretched hand, he broke his usual icy silence, and, emptying the

ROBESPIERRE

From a print in the Carnavalet Museum

vials of his righteous wrath on his visitor, he hurriedly dismissed him from the room.

But, in spite of all, the battle was not yet lost; the gauntlet had but been thrown down. Fouché, who still kept his spiritual predilection for feminine intervention, then remembered Charlotte, Robespierre's sister, who had once looked upon him with favour. The strollers in the Tuileries Gardens occasionally caught sight of a curious spectacle : the former Oratorian, as an amiable cavalier, paying his respects to the old maid ! But again in vain ! For if Charlotte really tried to influence her brother, her prayers had no effect on Robespierre's virtue.

It was difficult to find ways of achieving his end, but Fouché was not to be turned from his purpose until he had considered his position with the same methodical care as he had, in former days, shown for his physical laboratory in the school at Nantes. If the Convention at the present juncture was under Robespierre's control, the alternative must be to try to free from this same control his other mainstay, the Jacobin Club in Paris. Fouché hastened thither. He tried to ingratiate himself with the Jacobins by reading them the report over the Lyons proceedings, which had not yet been put before the Convention. Had he not proved his virtue when, in spite of Robespierre's threats, he had followed the dictates of his conscience and put an end to the wholesale slaughter in Lyons ? " My character cannot obey the changing winds of opinion ", was Fouché's unctuous justification, greeted by resounding applause. Robespierre, who was himself present, bit his lips, and at the moment could find no words with which to crush

F   81

Fouché's presumption. Fouché at first succeeded well in his efforts to save himself. He was even honoured with the chairmanship of the Club, a position which seemed to secure him from further persecution on the part of "the Incorruptible". Then Robespierre's authority increased still further. On the 20th of *Prairial*, according to the Revolution Calendar (June 8), a festival was held in the Tuileries Gardens in honour of the Supreme Being. Robespierre, in words that were evidently an indirect reflection on Fouché's former atheistic pronouncements, induced the Convention to proclaim their belief in God and a future life. The people were all gathered together, the men in great state wearing their swords and with oak-leaves in their hands, the women carrying bunches of roses and baskets of flowers. Fervent hymns were sung to the "Father of the Universe", whose temple is on the clouds, the mountains and the ocean waves. At last Robespierre stepped forward and, with his own hands, set fire to effigies of Atheism, Ambition, Egoism and Dissension. But there were also those who, branded by this ceremony, hid their bitter and sarcastic faces amongst the crowd. We can imagine we hear Fouché's quizzical voice whispering the words found in memoirs ascribed to him : What a fool this Robespierre is, "possessed by the ridiculous idea of giving a public acknowledgment of the existence of a Supreme Being ! "

The next act in the drama opened in the Jacobin Club. Robespierre showed no disposition whatever to leave Fouché alone, but, on the contrary, returned in the Club to the burning question of his devastations in the provinces. The threatening shadow of the scaffold loomed in the background, and Robespierre drew a picture of the divine justice which at last would hurl the bold sinner into the pit from which he had been dug. A deputation from plundered Nevers levelled their revengeful accusations at Fouché. He proved false in the hour of trial, and put up an unworthy defence by throwing the blame on his former comrade, Chaumette, who long since had been left lying at the place of execution. Now Robespierre's chance had come. "It is no use now to throw mud on Chaumette's grave, since this monster has already died upon the scaffold ; you ought to have fought him before his death." Fouché, who was not exactly an inspired orator, did not succeed in turning public opinion in his favour. He was, instead, challenged to answer for his actions, but did not appear, avoiding the hopeless contest. "He is afraid", Robespierre then burst out, " that his miserable face should be plain evidence of his crime, afraid that six thousand eyes, fastened upon him, should read in his eyes his inmost soul!" Fouché had irrevocably fallen from his high estate in the Club and was expelled from membership.

Again the Convention remained the last resort for the unhappy man. Fouché meantime was literally fighting for his life, nor did Robespierre underestimate his efforts. Overcome and driven on by fear, the Dictator exclaimed in the Jacobin Club: "I consider him the leader of the conspiracy which we have to thwart." But Fouché kept out of sight, avoided his home, creeping from door to door, with only the one message to each and all : " You are one of the favoured." People knew what he meant by this : each in his mind's eye saw himself in the executioner's cart. They listened and were afraid. For who knew where Robespierre's thunderbolt might next fall? His scattered opponents again joined hands, and the seats in the Convention were filled anew with mysteriously whispering crowds. *Thermidor* in the Revolution calendar was at hand.

To understand the final act in this drama we must fix our attention on the whole political situation, of which Fouché's undermining work formed only a part, even though possibly an important one. Robespierre had in May built up his edifice of power to a provocative height. By the side of the Committee of Public Welfare, the organization for the control of all matters that concerned government and the defence of the nation against enemies either within or without the country, there existed a Committee of Public Safety (*comité de sûreté générale*), with full powers to control the management of prisons, police and administration of the law. Now Robespierre had, in the first of these two Committees, set up on his own responsibility a special police bureau which was thought to have seriously encroached on the second Committee's sphere of authority. Also a measure for the reform of the revolutionary Tribunal had been carried through without consulting the Committee of Public Safety, thus rousing its members to a state of exasperation. The most dangerous among them was Vadier, a thin figure, tall but bent, with a sarcastic expression and the distinctive bearing of an old-fashioned official. The first suitable opportunity was seized for an attempt to represent Robespierre as an absurd, superstitious and narrow-minded man. He had also strained the patience of the

Convention to breaking-point when he had, in June 1794, compelled it to adopt a law giving to the Committees and the revolutionary Tribunal power on their own responsibility to arrest suspects amongst the members of the Convention, a decision which, however, the Convention at once rescinded in consequence of the vehement protests of the Opposition.

But there was also internal division in the Committee of Public Welfare. Carnot, celebrated as " the organizer of victory ", was offended at the interference of Robespierre's favourite, Saint-Just, in the conduct of the war. Opinions clashed, but Robespierre's vanity saw an accusation, a crime indeed, in every adverse criticism. How long would they be able to endure the tyrant's shameless arrogance ? Gradually the other members of the Committee began to flock round Carnot : Barère, who, after having constantly served Robespierre with the fine phrases of his weak eloquence, now played him false ; Billaud-Varennes, the inveterate terrorist, who was annoyed with Robespierre's despotic bearing ; and Collot d'Herbois, who still remembered his opposition to the rule of violence in Lyons. The atmosphere was therefore heavy with threatening storms, and became more and more electric from the rumours set afloat by the busy tongues of Fouché and his friends. " We shall see the traitors unmasked ", he wrote boldly to a friend. But at the same time Fouché tried to lull his opponents into security by secret negotiations with them.

Robespierre was also confident. He had, indeed, once for all, justice on his side, and justice must win in the Convention, which represented the virtuous and generous majesty of the nation. A miserable intriguer like Fouché had little weight there, nor a licentious man like this Tallien, who was driven to madness when his loved Thérèse Cabarras was taken before the revolutionary Tribunal. Yet the vague and ambiguous threats hurled forth from time to time by Robespierre and his friends during this growing and unbearable tension were imprudent, since they did but put weapons into the hands of the opposition. An end must be put, however, to the disorder. Robespierre rose to speak in the Convention on the 8th of *Thermidor*: " It would not be enough to purify the Convention, the Government must be purified as well." But not even then did he dare openly to denounce those whom he thought to be enemies of the Republic, not even Fouché.

Then all at once the storm broke over him from all sides, beginning in the Left's own ranks, and gradually re-echoing from the Centre and Right. Tallien led the attack, Collot d'Herbois supporting him in his position as President. Saint-Just, during the night that followed, made vain attempts to break up the opposition by denouncing Fouché before the Committee of Public Welfare as an unconscientious go-between. But Fouché shamelessly gave the lie to all such statements. At the same time the Jacobin Club vehemently espoused Robespierre's cause.

The storm burst the next day (July 27) in an order for the arrest and an indictment of Robespierre and his friends. But in his eyes all was not lost. Whilst under arrest he awaited with confidence the approaching trial, which, as he believed, would justify his virtue and prepare his triumph.

Meantime an unexpected happening took place. The Paris Commune took up arms, and the Convention at first stood powerless before their insurrection. Robespierre and his followers were—almost to their disappointment—set free, and by degrees gathered together in the Hôtel de Ville, the headquarters of the Commune. The insurrectionists wished to arrest those who had beguiled the Convention into such action against Robespierre. They did not at first think of Fouché in this connection, but, after Robespierre had come up to their help, his name was put upon the list as well. But they hesitated and deferred their attack upon the Convention, which then proceeded to a counter-attack, and succeeded in bringing over to their side great numbers of the armed population. The Convention troops at last stormed the Hôtel de Ville and brought back the prisoners. Their fate was soon sealed. Amidst the scorn and mockery of the mob, who had but lately cheered him to the echo, Robespierre passed over the same dark road which Danton had trodden before him. But Fouché, who all the time had been actively directing the proceedings from behind the scenes, was saved!

Chapter X

From Humiliation to Reinstatement

THE heroic age of the Republic had come to an end, that time of tragedy, of unutterable horror, of sufferings whose cry rose heaven-high. Party inquisitions continued, it is true, but the Convention deprived the Committee of Public Welfare of its supreme power. The instrument of death on the Place de la Concorde worked more and more slowly and intermittently, its place being taken by the "dry guillotine", viz. deportation and death amongst the swamps of Guiana. Plots and conspiracies were replaced by intrigues in the Convention corridors. Unpretentious democratic simplicity no longer had any charm for men who had lost their illusions, and, in its stead, luxury and elegance became the fashion, whilst dancing to the strains of a noisy band was soon to be seen in hundreds of places in Paris that not long before had re-echoed to the measured tread and solemn hymns of their fellow-citizens in sad and slow procession. The background behind this apparent festivity, however, grew darker and darker, with high prices, poverty and the anarchy existing in the surrounding country. Bands of robbers ran riot where, before the Convention, Representatives, with their brutal methods, had enforced public order and discipline. Punishment without mercy was dealt out to the now defenceless Jacobins in revenge for their past misdeeds. The Royalists began to show signs of life, and Vendée once more became a destructive canker in the Republican State. But already, through the whirl of gaiety and general confusion, glimpses could be caught of the powers that the morrow was to bring, fierce and haughty soldiers from the victorious republican armies in Belgium and along the Rhine, the henchmen of liberty on the field of battle, and with them, too, the guardians of order behind the fighting lines. No one knew what was coming. The fate of the Republic was in the melting-pot.

In Fouché's life these were years of sad humiliation. He had not intended, any more than the other conspirators, to put an end to the Terror when he fought against Robespierre. They all lived under the firm conviction of the impassable gulf that existed between the regicides' Republic and the rest of France. Fouché again became a member of the Jacobin Club, and there proposed as a watchword " the necessity of striking terror into the hearts of the ill-disposed as well as into the camps of the enemy ". He did not even give up his old plans of establishing general economic equality. Babeuf, the pioneer of French Socialism, who was now definitely entering the arena, could rely upon his assistance. Whilst cries of woe still continued to rise from Nevers and Lyons, Fouché, however, tried to wriggle out of the difficulty in a very suspicious way. He pretended to take the part of Lyons, alleging as proof the charity which, he insisted, he had practised during the last months of his stay there, and laid all the blame for the carnage on Collot d'Herbois. To divert attention from himself Fouché took a very active part in the accusations brought against another of the

89

Convention's Representatives on Mission, Carrier, who had tortured the unfortunate inhabitants of the town of Nantes.

But Fouché's enemies did not cease their attacks. His position became noticeably worse after the seventy-three Girondists, who had been driven out of the Convention in June 1793, took their seats again in the spring of 1795. The popular insurrections in Paris during April and May at last utterly destroyed his influence in politics, whether he had had a share in them or not. The summer of 1795 turned out a time of reaction, and in August the Convention, after lengthy debates, decided that Fouché should be arrested. It is true the resolution was not carried out, for Fouché, as usual, made successful intrigues with those in power, but at the same time his election as member of the National Assembly, which in the autumn of 1795 took the place of the Convention, was forbidden, and this prohibition afterwards held good. Thus Fouché found himself with his family in the deplorable position of a discredited professional politician without a constituency or public service. In addition, his private means had disappeared. The negro plantations in San Domingo, which he had inherited, had gone after the slave-riots that had broken out there in 1792, and his properties in Brittany had become utterly valueless as a result of their destruction in the frequent Royalist disturbances. Everything now seemed lost. Neither—to his honour be it said—had he anything left over from his activity as a Convention Representative in the provinces.

But in the midst of his pecuniary straits he acted, to

begin with, in a manner that reminds one of the Spanish proverb, " Even if your pocket is empty, see your hat is straight ", for no sooner had the order for his arrest been passed than he wrote an open letter to the members of the Convention in which, amongst other things, he said : " Kings have no friends among you. They will ask for your surrender one after another. They will by no means pardon your numerous services. You set up liberty. They will never forget that you are the founders and passionate lovers of the Republic."

These were words bearing witness to political insight, for they took into account the dominating feature of the situation. The organization of the Republic might be altered, the absolute authority of the Convention exchanged for a division of power between the Government and the representative public assembly as well as between the two chambers of this assembly which distinguished the subsequent constitution of the Directory (*Directoire*), but the " regicides " of 1793 had no intention of relinquishing their power. The main body of the members of the Convention had secured for themselves a place in the national representation, and they prepared themselves to uphold the Republic against the fugitive Bourbon dynasty and its supporters in the country no less than against the attempts of foreign Powers to overthrow it. But now they were occupied with politics and refrained from moral judgments.

The danger, however, was past for Fouché, after the party of the Left, on October 5 (*Vendémiaire*), had succeeded in putting down a Royalist insurrection in Paris. " The cannon of *Vendémiaire*, directed by Bonaparte, gave back to me, in many respects, liberty and honour ", so runs an entry in Fouché's memoirs. But his circumstances were just as straightened as before. His only friend in misfortune was Vicomte Barras, who in the Convention had helped to bring about Robespierre's fall, and now occupied a place in the new Constitution, the Directory. He was a deserter from the old nobility, an unconscientious political gambler, who backed the Revolution horse, and in due time took home his winnings in the shape of power, money and enjoyment. Yet Barras was, too, a well-bred man who duly honoured old ties of friendship, so he got Fouché a couple of chance political appointments, but, as they were far away from Paris, they did not much improve matters for him either.

Fouché was now living—if Barras's memoirs are to be believed—lodged with his family in a wretched old building in Paris. Little Nièvre had pined away in the arms of her broken-hearted father in the midst of those stormy *Thermidor* days. But his cup of sorrow was not yet full. During these hard years two more children were born, both of whom died at a tender age. Fouché tried to keep the wolf from the door by becoming a business-man like everyone else in the time of the Directory. With another ex-member of the Convention, Fouché—so Barras relates—began rearing pigs. His partner advanced the money to buy a number of little pigs, and Fouché fattened them so effectively that in a short time they could be sold at double their cost. But then the partners had a difference of opinion. Fouché, who had originated the idea, wanted the lion's share of the profits, whilst the other thought he had a right to the first claim since he was the financier of the enterprise. A scandalous lawsuit was impending between the two former members of the Convention, when Barras is said to have intervened as arbitrator. Fouché also tried detective work on a small scale, an occupation in which he soon felt at home. In spite of his extreme poverty, however, he by his own actions made his presence in the Paris Government undesirable, and he was banished in December 1795 to the Montmorency Valley, away in the country. This was, indeed, to reach the depths of his degradation, a hard lesson that taught him for ever that a politician's first care must be his own pecuniary welfare.

When Fouché, at the beginning of 1797, was able to return to Paris, he succeeded in starting a company for the delivery of provisions to the troops which the French had concentrated on the north-west coast. He afterwards got rid of his partners, and by his own efforts laid the foundation of his prosperity, of which the first farthings were probably much more hardly earned than millions of francs later on. After this Fouché continued " to make up for lost time "—his own expression—helped the great financier, Hinguerlot, in a difficulty which had landed him before the Tribunal in Melun, increased his connections with the inner circle of the Paris private bankers, and further enriched himself by contraband trade on the Dutch frontiers. He was no longer, as in Nevers and Lyons, a keen supporter of a democratic simplicity with " bread and iron" as its only resources, but attached far more importance to the amount of his credit balance and to his lucrative connections with the *nouveaux-riches* members of the middle class.

Fouché did not, however, give up his political intrigues. He was disturbed in 1797 by the general deflection to the Right, which attracted his attention, and for a moment made him think that the dreaded Restoration was imminent. He appears to have been seized by panic, and perhaps it was his apprehension that drove him to try to get into touch with the Comte de Provence—afterwards Louis XVIII—in order, as far as he was concerned, to save all that could possibly be saved. At any rate, Fouché made advances in the Royalist direction. He was met by coolness; the regicide was not considered suitable as a king-maker—a lesson Fouché did not soon forget. He made his choice, however, and supported instead—with a typical change of front—to the utmost of his power the movement to the Left which in September (*Fructidor*) 1797 cleared out of the Representative Committees and the Directory all the Royalistic element. In due course the Royalists would have reason to regret their cool attitude towards Fouché—as Robespierre had had to do before them.

Meantime he was now once more a power to be reckoned with. In September 1798 his friend, Director Barras, was successful in securing Fouché's appointment as French Ambassador in the Cisalpine Republic, i.e. in Northern Italy, which, in 1796, had been freed by General Bonaparte from Austrian supremacy. Fouché grasped the situation in the twinkling of an eye. In his opinion it was not fitting that France should assume the attitude of ruler towards the surrounding protected States, the five newly formed republics, control them by her officials and soldiers, drain them of men and

94

necessaries, and thus make capital out of the ideals of the Revolution. This was but to foster feelings of hostility and revenge. It was advisable, rather, by the exercise of a wise and imperceptible influence, to bring about by degrees the universal triumph of the Republican flag. This was a liberal attitude quite in keeping with that which he had wished to adopt in 1792 towards the Royalist priests, and a clever policy as well. He therefore brought about in Milan a *coup d'état* which put into power the Italian party for independence. In this he had the valuable support of the manly young General Joubert, the hope of France, who had been made Commander-in-Chief of the forces there. But the majority in the French Government disapproved of Fouché's generous attitude. He was dismissed, and was almost compelled to hasten back to France. When, however, in the spring of 1799 the Russians and Austrians invaded Northern Italy, France bitterly regretted that she had not followed Fouché's prudent advice and kept on friendly terms with the Italians.

At the same time the Russians and English prepared to attack France's northern dependent State, the Batavian Republic in Holland, where French and Dutch now had to combine in its defence. The task was not easy, for the native Batavian Government dreaded French oppression as much as English supremacy, represented in the country by the Jacobin and Orange parties respectively. In July, Fouché was appointed French Ambassador in Holland, and the Dutch Government, as the result of his influence and authority, in a short time broke entirely with the Orange party, and their

General, Daendels, placed his forces at the disposal of Brune, the French Commander-in-Chief.

Fouché had won his spurs as a diplomatist. He appears secretly to have looked upon diplomacy as his future mission in life. Meantime he received an express message from Paris announcing his appointment as Minister of Police.

Chapter XI

The Valued Official of the Directoire

THE republican ship of State, which had before threatened to founder as a result of violent heeling to starboard, had now got a serious list to port. It was no longer the Right but the Jacobins who attempted to turn aside from the contemplated course. By means of a new *coup d'état*, in June (*Prairial*) 1799, the liberty of meeting had been extended, and, as a result, a wild growth of voluble Jacobin Clubs had sprung into existence. The extreme Left had, at the same time, acquired two deputies in the Directory, the lawyer Gohier and General Moulin, both equally insignificant individuals. It was on good terms, too, with the War Minister, Bernadotte, and the Commandant in Paris, General Marbot. We find amongst the Directors, too, Roger Ducos and his confidant Siéyès, the veteran of the Revolution, who as far back as 1789 had vindicated the rights of the People, the " Third Estate ". Siéyès was a believer in secret policy, and viewed the State through the magnifying glass of constitutional theories, just as a watchmaker inspects a watch through his lens. He also brought in some degree to his political speculation the boundless professional pride of a craftsman and some of his economic thrift as well.

The fifth Director, Barras, describes Siéyès's relation to him by saying that if only Siéyès was applauded for his utterances, Barras could practically do whatever he wished. That evil must be expelled by evil was, in July 1799, the joint opinion of Barras and Siéyès about the Jacobins. They must therefore be mastered by Fouché, who was to be made Minister of Police. This was a newly created office, hitherto without any political weight and with little authority over the motley and despised crowd of police agents, who acted on their own initiative and contented themselves with an occasional written communication to their chief. How Fouché gradually controlled this machinery with his iron hand in a velvet glove shall be related in another connection. Quick as lightning he set up, in August 1799, an independent authority in opposition to the Directory. The latter authority were amazed when Fouché began with a blow at the Right by proposing to take harsher measures against those who had been compromised in the *Fructidor coup d'état*. " When will the Jacobins' turn come ? " inquired Siéyès. " To-morrow ", was Fouché's reply. But first it was essential to take precautions against being stamped as reactionaries. The Directory submitted to this just as, immediately after, on Fouché's initiative, it proposed to the Council to confine the liberty of meeting to purely private discussions.

The second chamber—the Council of The Five Hundred —was furious, and spoke of Fouché's past in the same disrespectful terms as in the days of the Convention. The proposed law did not meet with approval, but Fouché carried out his policy none the less. Shortly after the Jacobin Club in the Rue du Bac, in the midst of a consultative meeting, was honoured by an unexpected visit. Fouché in person deigned to carry out the work of a simple police officer. The meeting was

98

quite taken aback and protested, but soon found it wise to disperse. It was their last meeting, for Fouché had the keys in his pocket when he calmly returned to his office in the Hôtel de Juigné, on the Quai Voltaire. He was not content with half-measures, and the next to go was the Commandant in Paris himself, General Marbot, who, at Fouché's instigation, was replaced by General Lefèbre, a man of honour, well known as the husband of Madame Sans-Gêne. The Minister of War, Bernadotte, did not hear of the matter until it had occurred. He himself is supposed to have received some trying exhortations from Fouché, and soon shared Marbot's fate, being manœuvred out of his post by Siéyès. The Press criticized in no measured terms, and Fouché suppressed eleven newspapers, organs of Left and Right alike.

In all this was Fouché as faithless to the Revolution as he had been during his intrigues of 1797? He himself undoubtedly considered he was doing it a service, since the Jacobins of 1799 showed themselves to be nothing but an unrestrained blustering crowd who by their foolishness might work into the hands of the Royalist reactionaries. What then was the aim of Fouché's policy? First and foremost, certainly, to ward off a revenge for his terroristic misdeeds. Probably he was influenced in it by his memories of the year 1797. The Royalist Powers were implacable, and the Terror, which had just ended, would not begin again under the banner of the fleur-de-lis. For in such a case poor France must perish in the fires and counter-fires whose flames would scorch her again and again. To this must be added another thought to which Fouché afterwards occasionally gave frank expression. A restoration of the Bourbon power would certainly bring with it an economic revolution in France. For the returning *émigrés* would endeavour to get back their extensive properties, which had been confiscated during the Revolution, and in great measure had come into the possession of the new peasant-proprietors' class. It was, then, not only essential to protect the poorer classes against such danger to their prosperity, but also to prevent the nobility from again acquiring such an economic position as would practically make them the rulers of France. If the Jacobins, in their want of common sense, ever risked a Royalist reaction, they never escaped the punishment meted out to them by Fouché's indignation.

From the very first Fouché took the policy against the Royalists into his own hands. By means of trusted underlings he kept an ever-watchful eye on the seething unrest in la Vendée, which since 1793 had so often burst out and died down again, and he showed no mercy in his dealings with the disturbers of the peace. But he no longer thought as before that such a deep-seated and chronic unrest could be suppressed by forcible means alone. It must be kept within bounds, conquered by care and patience, leavened by police supervision and controlled from within. The nobility were not nearly such fanatics as the Royalist peasants, and Fouché acted like a fatherly pedagogue to all who reformed and became converts to the new order of things. He pardoned everything but forgot nothing, and kept former mischief-makers under continuous observation. If they proved backsliders, Fouché never failed to use the methods he had formerly adopted when Representative of the Convention, viz. those of guile and force.

*   *   *   *   *

Meantime the position was an impossible one : a group of despised or compromised professional politicians at the head of a democratic Government, in which national elections were the order of the day, and which was daily becoming more and more completely surrounded by fierce external enemies. Bonaparte, whose triumphant flourish of trumpets had three years earlier united and encouraged France, was at this juncture unable to help, as he was far away with an army in distant Egypt. The name of General Joubert—with whose efficiency Fouché had become acquainted in Italy—was for a moment on everyone's lips as the man of the day, but as early as August 1799 his gallant career was ended by a musket-shot at Novi. Could it be possible that France would shortly be compelled to seek pardon for her crimes at the feet of the Bourbons ? Barras was really prepared to relinquish the struggle and throw down his cards. Fouché quite naturally looked upon such a prospect with repugnance.

Chapter XII

The Weather-Cock in St. Cloud

JUST as Fouché, four years before, had modestly tried to win Charlotte Robespierre's favour in order to get into her dreaded brother's good graces, so now again his dark figure was to be seen in the circle of empty-headed admirers that surrounded Bonaparte's charming wife, Josephine. The allowance which she regularly received from Bonaparte was not nearly enough to cover the cost of the gay fêtes that filled her days and nights. With a father confessor's keen insight, Fouché saw the state of affairs. Personally he was not much affected by the troubles of the frivolous woman, but was it not worth a pretty penny to get a glimpse of the first-hand news that she received now and then from Egypt? He found no difficulty whatever in making an arrangement of such an apparently innocent nature. It proved the beginning of a curious alliance which lasted for years, and from the very first secured Fouché a position as Josephine's ally in her violent disputes with her husband's mother, brothers and sisters.

Then, all at once, the ominous calm was broken. Something like an electric shock passed through Paris. Bonaparte was on French soil. A strong Government would have made short work of a General who had left his army adrift in Egypt, but, as we have said, the Directory was but a weak reed. Moreover, a storm of applause greeted Bonaparte on his arrival, beginning with the working and middle classes, who hoped to get peace and quiet for their work through him, and extending even to the celebrated scientists in Paris, who admired the man with the iron will, so immeasurably superior to the feeble gentlemen of the *Directoire*. It was too much for the young and inexperienced soldier. His head was turned by the sudden popularity, and he began to dream of being lifted to the heights of power by the flaming enthusiasm of the entire nation. He overlooked the fact that he had first to break the solid and stubborn opposition of the party-men who clung to the reforms of the constitution, and who, moreover, literally lived on their profession as politicians. It is true the frequent *coups d'état* had taught them to respect military weapons, but they did not understand the Romanesque idealism displayed by Bonaparte, and suspected it was but a blind for terrible schemes for absolute power. This idea grew stronger when Bonaparte at times involuntarily changed his tones and uttered his habitual short words of command. There was no lack of indignation either in the military circles, where they were annoyed at the failure in discipline of which Bonaparte had been guilty when he deserted his army. They sympathized, moreover, with the politicians of the Left, who were eager that the Revolution war should be fought to a finish, whilst Bonaparte's position was that of an advocate for peace.

In the midst of all these intrigues a reconciliation took place between Josephine and Napoleon Bonaparte. The thirty-year-old General, who had before wished for a divorce from his faithless wife, again fell under the spell of Josephine's wit and exquisite charm. Fouché could, from his place in Josephine's box, get a good view of the preparations for the play ! It was not long before he was having free intercourse with all the actors from highest to lowest. Now, if ever, Fouché played a ghost-like part, invisible, yet omnipresent, informed on every point, whilst himself free and unfettered. But he took good care not to take an active part in the performance, for he saw that the different rôles were mainly in the hands of political dilettanti who might easily be hissed off the stage. Perhaps, too, Fouché was also influenced by respect for his former protector, Barras, who irresolutely kept out of the whole business. In short, Fouché contented himself with being, as Minister of Police, blind and deaf to what was going on, at the same time seeing that public order was maintained in the Paris streets and squares. We must also mention that, according to Napoleon's own words, Fouché was the only one who, before the *coup*, had given him reliable information about people and conditions.

A writer of memoirs relates two amusing tales touching Fouché's mysterious attitude during these days of preparation. If they are not true, they are, at any rate, *ben trovato*. On one occasion Fouché invited several of the conspirators to his house. Only a couple of them knew that he was one of the initiated. Judge then of the others' amazement when they scanned one another in Fouché's drawing-room and felt themselves helplessly at his mercy. Two days before the *coup d'état*, General Bonaparte gave a great reception at which one of those present was the Director Gohier, a man of honour, who was quite uninitiated and had no suspicion of any

REVOLUTIONARY COMMITTEE UNDER THE TERROR, 1793–1794

From an old print by Fragonard

treachery. "What is the news, Citizen Minister?" he asked Fouché. "Nothing but the same idle talk", Fouché replied, "only that conspiracy." There was an outburst of amazement and protestation, but Fouché soothed their anxiety. "Trust to me. They won't catch me napping." Gohier informed Josephine, the lady of his heart, in a satisfied whisper that the Minister of Police was certainly the man for his post, and that she might sleep in peace. But Josephine, who to the accompaniment of Napoleon's ironical applause was only playing with honest Gohier, merely laughed in her sleeve.

Siéyès and Napoleon stood side by side as the chief movers in the scheme, and they also had the support of their friend, Roger Ducos, the Director. Their plan was this : First to dissolve the Directory. The Council of Seniors, who had the right to determine the place for the Council's meeting, was to transfer it to the royal country palace of St. Cloud, near Paris, and at the same time give Bonaparte control over the capital. In St. Cloud the Council of The Five Hundred, with their undoubted Jacobin majority, would not have the Paris crowd rushing to their side, but would instead be liable to military restraint. The Councils were thus to pass a statute enacting that, for the present, the Government was to be vested in three "Consuls", Bonaparte, Siéyès and Roger Ducos.

It was a plan full of gaps and uncertainties in which the weakest point was that it had to be carried through in two different stages. What might not happen between? Since the enterprise was, of course, to be accomplished under colour of the Council's approval,

the majority in the Council of The Five Hundred
assumed a significance that might have disastrous con-
sequences.

But the conspirators could not give up the idea that
the sovereignty of the people—even if only represented
by the despised councils of the Directory régime—must
in one way or another be decisive on this occasion too.
Yet the Royalists had, indeed, in 1797 hoped to win the
majority in the Councils, and so to be able to raise
Louis XVIII to the French throne, hopes that at first
seemed in a fair way to fulfilment, but in September of
the same year were brought to ruin by the *Fructidor
coup d'état.*

On *Brumaire* 18 (November 8) Fouché was awakened
by two spies, who eagerly told him the Council of Seniors
had passed the resolution agreed upon. Fouché now
made preparations to appear as the surprised and per-
plexed Minister of Police. He hurried to the Luxemburg
Palace, the headquarters of the Directory, where he
found Gohier and Moulin very depressed, whilst their
colleague, Barras, was keeping out of the way in his
private room. Gohier greeted Fouché with a well-
deserved flood of reproaches. Was he by any chance
appearing now as the herald of the " Council of
Seniors " ? How had he fulfilled his duty of informing
the Directory of the criminal conspiracy that was being
planned ? Fouché answered by boldly hinting that it
was the Directory themselves who had been the cause
of it all. Had not Siéyès and Roger Ducos joined the
Council of the Seniors ?

Fouché, now decided on his course of action, went to
his office, had the city gates closed and a strict watch

kept in quarters where disturbances might be feared. Then he went to see Bonaparte, who with all pomp and state was just making his début as head of a rebellion, surrounded by a crowd of enthusiastic followers. The General was intoxicated with success, and Fouché got, in passing, a reproof for his blockade precautions. The popular following and enthusiasm surely showed that Bonaparte was acting in the name of the nation. All went well too—that day. Barras formally resigned his office as Director. Gohier and Moulin were shut up in the Luxemburg under the charge of General Moreau, a brilliant and loyal soldier, who had resigned before Bonaparte's daring deed, and now sat, pipe in mouth, awaiting coming events.

In the evening, however, evil forebodings began to worry Siéyès. Who knew what the noisy mischief-makers in the Council of The Five Hundred might decide to do before the morrow? The assembly, to be sure, had at their disposal a guard of grenadiers. But if these took the side of the majority of The Five Hundred, Bonaparte's troops might easily be carried away by their example. Ever since the fall of the Girondists, force of arms had always given the decisive verdict in *coups d'état*. Siéyès, therefore, proposed to Bonaparte to end all uncertainty by at once arresting the most fiery of the Jacobin hot-heads. But Bonaparte turned a deaf ear. He meant to conquer by the magic power of his personality. Perhaps he imagined that in such case he would also be the only one to gather the fruits of victory. Fouché, who was present, possibly encouraged the General in his obstinacy, for he would be quite pleased to have a hand in humiliating the pompous Siéyès. On the other hand, he was certainly confirmed in his caution by the divisions and disorder in the ranks of the conspirators.

Next day, the ominous 19th of *Brumaire*, when the political centre of gravity was all at once moved out beyond the gates of Paris, Fouché calmly remained in the city. His conduct on this occasion gave rise a little later on to a joke that attracted much attention in the comedy, " The Weather-Cock in St. Cloud " : Mr. Tourniquet has put on the battlements of the castle a boy, Furet, who by means of a cleverly arranged weather-cock announces the course of events during the *coup d'état*, and, in accordance with the varying indications, Mr. Tourniquet makes nimble changes in his words and plans ; at three in the afternoon he is a Jacobin, at 5 p.m. a Bonapartist. The Police Minister's " Furet " was, as a matter of fact, Fouché's general secretary, Thurot, and from him Fouché actually did receive a report every half-hour from St. Cloud. But, since facts are stranger than fiction, these clever arrangements threatened to end in disaster for Fouché himself. Thurot endeavoured to get into favour with Bonaparte at Fouché's expense, and in the end, by his own agents, to take over the guardianship of Paris into his own hands ; but he was frustrated by his superior officer, and afterwards lost, in his turn, his post. Fouché, in common with most jokers, evidently had no liking for jokes at his own expense.

But even apart from this little interlude, *Brumaire* 19 was an anxious day for Fouché. The intention had been that the Councils should meet at noon in their respective rooms, but unfortunately the carpenters and paperhangers had not finished their work by then, with the result that the members of the two councils were all mixed together as they waited. The Five Hundred watched their opportunity to upbraid the Seniors for their revolutionary action and to terrify them with warnings of Bonaparte's ideas of a dictatorship. When the meeting at last began, everything seemed to go wrong for the conspirators. Bonaparte failed to induce the Council of the Seniors to give a clear pronouncement in favour of a national revolution. When he tried his luck with the Council of The Five Hundred, he was met by abuse and had to take refuge in flight. The Council's grenadiers looked upon him with mistrust, and his own troops hesitated to interfere. It was his brother Lucien, who fortunately filled the position of President of the meeting, who quite unexpectedly settled the matter. When he, too, was attacked by abuse, he gave a dramatic turn to the proceedings by suddenly declaring that his parliamentary dignity was insulted, made a successful appeal to the grenadiers, and put himself at the head of an armed attack on the unruly Jacobin majority, who were scattered like chaff before the wind. By this stroke of luck, which was cleverly utilized by Napoleon, the victory was won. Without further difficulties the remnant of the Council approved of everything that the conspirators desired. Fouché, who had held himself in readiness to shut out a defeated Bonaparte from Paris, now had the pleasure of greeting him on his entry as a victorious conqueror.

In this way, however, the *Brumaire coup* did not bring about any violent change as the result of the revolutionary disturbances. Bonaparte did not become, as he himself

hoped, the man who came, saw and conquered, not the
" god of the day ", to use his own romantic expression,
which reminds us rather of an Oriental figure of speech
than of the phrases of the French Revolution. All that
had taken place was a *coup d'état* much like those of
Vendémiaire and *Fructidor*. Now, as then, by the side
of the soldiers we catch a glimpse of old familiar faces
from the Convention times. As before, no one knew
what the morrow might bring—if obedience would
have to be rendered to the rule of several politicians or
of one military commander.

Fouché, who with his keen political insight was quick
to perceive the drift of current events, began, however,
to suspect that Napoleon, in spite of all, was the man
who would be able to ward off the restoration of the
Monarchy and maintain the work of the Revolution in
France. His expectations were to be realized beyond
his dreams.

PART II

FOUCHÉ, NAPOLEON AND LOUIS XVIII

Chapter XIII

Fouché and Bonaparte

THE *Brumaire coup*, carried through with such irresolution and confusion, was quickly justified by its results. The weak directorial Government was replaced by rulers who knew their aims and carried them out with determination—the three Consuls, with Bonaparte, the leading spirit, as First Consul, all appointed for ten years. The Republic seemed to be saved. There was no longer any competition for its legacy of power. On the other hand, it did not appear that any absolute individual rule was predominant under the outward forms of Republicanism, for the continuance of the Constitution was to be secured by a Senate, replaced, it is true, by the Consuls at first, but afterwards to be brought up to its full numbers under certain restrictions ; the legislative power was to be vested in two newly appointed assemblies, the Tribunal and the Legislative Council, both elected by the Senate. The exhausted French nation began to hope for internal quiet and external peace now that the work of the Revolution seemed to be assured in all its essential points. The new Constitution decreed, moreover, that the lands belonging to the *émigrés* and the Church should remain in the possession of the State. But that also meant that the very many private individuals who had bought such State lands would be able to feel secure from any after-reckonings on behalf of the former owners. General Bonaparte soon dismissed Siéyès and his worn-out theories from power and influence; Cambacérès and Lebrun remained at his side as Consuls. Fouché, too, was kept on as Minister of Police, for he was now a popular guardian in the eyes of all sober-minded republicans. He had, namely, immediately after the *coup d'état* quite boldly in his own name issued a number of circulars and public announcements in which he declared that the Republic had been preserved in its entirety, that the weak could now feel safe from violence under the protection of the Government, that all could calmly return to their own affairs, that the Royalists' hopes were completely vanquished, and that the Government would give protection to all and undue favour to none. To discharge the Minister of Police would have meant risking the prestige of the new ruling powers among wide circles of the public.

Thus Napoleon Bonaparte and Fouché began their work together, that stern trial of strength between passions and genius on the one hand, and cold, far-sighted calculation, overweening lust of power and unscrupulous political activity, on the other.

Fouché certainly was changed in a moment from the loyal official of the Directory to the no less trusty servant of Bonaparte, but this change scarcely brought with it, as far as he was concerned, any change either in his political views or even in his political action. The very fact that he was a veteran of the Revolution made him of use and value in the new Government. As long as he was Minister of Police the Consuls considered that they had in him a much-needed scourge to ensure the Jacobin party's good behaviour. His ruthless attitude to this party during the summer of 1799 could, it is

114

true, not erase the memory that he had voted for the execution of Louis XVI and had worked as a Terrorist in Lyons. With his usual keenness of perception and quick adaptability, Fouché realized this fact, and, making a virtue of necessity, he liked to pose to those in authority as a representative of the Jacobins. This policy was and could not fail to be his, but, as far as his own private feelings were concerned, he had been too deeply involved in the bloodthirsty mistakes of the Reign of Terror and had suffered too much loss from party persecutions to continue to be a whole-hearted champion of the revolutionary programme. No one had learnt by more bitter experience that " stern masters do not rule long ", and that their stern rule at last is meted out to themselves. No one knew better how prosaic and inferior the individual factors of a parliamentary majority could be than did Fouché, who had once united a terrified and vindictive Convention to the attack on Robespierre. A lesson of a more positive kind, dating from revolutionary times, found expression in Fouché's opinion that the public newspapers ought to give unqualified support to those in power. Thus he remarked on one occasion (1818) that when a journalist utters but one word of attack, ten pages are required for an effectual defence, and " a Minister has something better to do ". He preferred to guide public opinion himself. Fouché, who in the past had defended his principles with such impetuosity and ostentation, now laid his political mines in silence and darkness, and from a safe and inconspicuous place watched to see if they had the desired effect.

It was certainly a superstition when Bonaparte saw in Fouché a terrifying and hampering embodiment of the very spirit of the Revolution, but there was a certain truth in it as well. Fouché, irrevocably allied as he was by his past and his crimes with the legacy of the Revolution and the fate of those who had brought it about, had, with ruthless calm, observed and tested the means adopted and the objects pursued by Revolutionists at different times. He had seen through their prejudices and poses and learnt to perceive human corruptibility and forgetfulness, passions and sensuality. Sympathetic tolerance was now the distinguishing mark of his worldly philosophy, cynical calculation the stamp on his statecraft. Events soon pass—wise is the man who calmly bides his time ! But is there any greater stupidity than to stand in discouraged amazement and let a happy chance slip by ? So Fouché stood prepared to meet the new time—" with a heart of diamond, a stomach of iron and a tearless eye ", to quote Talleyrand's description.

If Fouché was thus the clear-sighted heir of the Revolution, General Bonaparte was a new-comer on the political arena. His enthusiastic admirer and biographer, Frédéric Masson, in a lecture during 1908, gave a striking picture of the young Corsican's first experiences on French soil. Imagine a young, noble-hearted Frenchman, brought up in Alsace-Lorraine under German rule, who was graciously sent to barren Prussia to be trained as a soldier in the conqueror's army, far away from his sunny native land ! How he must have felt his schoolfellows' arrogance, with what lonely desperation he must have dreamt of being one day able at last to fight for the sacred cause of France ! Such were the sufferings, tortures even, of Napoleon Bonaparte, the reserved and

116

dreamy Corsican, whose beloved native island had been subdued by the French, and who now, thanks to his father's enjoyment of the royal favour, was trained as a French officer in the military school at Brienne. Then the Revolution threw open the lists to his indomitable will.

So far Masson. Even Bonaparte was certainly stirred by the force and violence of the Reign of Terror. The very fact that he remained unfamiliar with French soil made him look upon the Revolution as a mysterious volcanic movement that affected men's minds as inexorably as any natural law. But he soon perceived that Revolutionists were seldom on a level with the mighty movements that shook the times. Long after, he still smiled at the memory of the " General " Doppet who was his commanding officer at the siege of rebellious Toulon—that spokesman in the Jacobin Club, a doctor by profession, who hated all talents and before the enemy's fire raved over the aristocrats' treacherous attack. Amidst the crowd of frightened and irresolute incapables Bonaparte's sovereign will soon made its way. " Reward and promote this young man, for if we are ungrateful to him he will find promotion by his own efforts ", was the testimonial he received after his achievements at Toulon from General Dugommier, a soldier of the good old school.

It was not long before Bonaparte fulfilled this prophecy. The soldiers' increasing political influence during the Directory gave his ambition an opportunity to spread its wings. His own brilliant feats of strategy in Italy placed him in the front ranks of the Republican generals. Not even his disasters in Egypt could shake his self-reliance. After the *Brumaire* days his name acted like a lodestar on the whole French nation.

From the *Brumaire coup* onwards, Bonaparte's constant and steadfast determination was to break down the barriers that party hatred had raised between people of different opinions, to respect the religious feelings of the poorer classes, which had been wounded by the atheists of the Terror, and to grant to all loyal members of society full rights of citizenship, irrespective of their political views. These aims were the source not only of his want of sympathy with the former internal dissensions, but also of his strength. But the deep-rooted differences persisted. When Napoleon made a gesture of reconciliation to the Royalists, they wondered if it was not his intention to fulfil their dearest wishes and to restore what, in their opinion, was the only lawful dynasty. The former royal house of the Bourbons also hastened to find out his opinions and plans at once. They were met by an opposition no less passionate and determined than any from the regicides' camp. What had the Corsican in common with Royalist dreams and memories ? The answers he gave to the Bourbons and their emissaries show most markedly Bonaparte's limitations and peculiarities of temperament. On one occasion after *Brumaire*—so Ernest Daudet relates—Bonaparte had an interview with a representative of the Royalist rebels in France, d'Andigné. They discussed amicably questions concerning peace and reconciliation, when d'Andigné ventured to hint that Bonaparte ought to put his power at the disposal of the claimant to the throne, Louis XVIII. Bonaparte flared up : " The Bourbons have no more prospects. They have done nothing for the sake of honour. Why were they not in la Vendée? That was their place." When d'Andigné tried to represent, in reply, that the policy of the Foreign Powers had prevented the princes from crossing the English Channel to assist their French followers who were fighting the Republican soldiers, back came the reply : " They ought to have thrown themselves into a fishing-boat ". What were hoary traditions to him, " the son of mighty deeds ", when an inherited position was not vindicated by personal valour? Bonaparte went on to make a warm appeal to d'Andigné and his companions to throw in their lot with the new order of things in France. " Join the side where honour is to be found. Come to our standards. My government is to be the government of youth and genius. You and yours shall become whatever you wish." Bonaparte's words struck no answering note. Neither his commanding presence and charm nor his decisive pronouncements were able to induce all persons and things alike to fall down at his feet. He failed in his attempt to bridge the gulf between the French Republic of the regicides and the French Fatherland of the Royalists.

Time passed by. Victory followed Bonaparte's banners, and a general European peace crowned his successes. His power was even more firmly established when, in the spring of 1802, he received the position of First Consul for life, with the right to name his successor. The work of the Revolution seemed to find full completion under his powerful protection, whilst the Bourbons apparently had less prospect than ever of regaining the throne of their fathers. Was this not a reason why, before they entirely disappeared,

the Bourbons should come to an honourable agreement
with Bonaparte?

At the suggestion of Czar Alexander, Bonaparte
himself took the first step in such a direction and offered
to the Bourbons, through the mediation of the Prussian
King, generous, economic compensation if only they
would formally renounce all their claims to the French
throne. But the unfortunate, exiled King, Louis XVIII,
did not yield in spite of all. "As descendant of the
saintly Louis", he said, "I must follow his example
and consider my dignity even in chains. As successor
to Francis I, I wish at least to be able to say with him:
We have lost all but honour." Thus he weighed the
mighty perspective of history against the moment's
need. How small General Bonaparte appeared in the
brilliant light of the great and imperishable heritage of
the royal house of France!

The contrast was indeed striking, even glaring. But
Bonaparte picked up the glove with all a soldier's
bravado. The chief of his secret police, Desmarest,
tells us that the First Consul scornfully showed him the
Bourbon's answer with the words: "This is the
document in which Louis XVIII, who has never drawn
the sword, sets up Saint-Louis and Francis I against me,
the avenger of Saint-Louis on the Mamelukes and of
Francis I at Pavia." What puppet shows were Saint-
Louis' crusades in comparison with but one of Bonaparte's conflicts under the shadow of the Pyramids!
What a poor figure the pompous Francis cut by the
side of the little broad-shouldered Corporal, taking up
the cudgels for his grenadiers on the bridge at Arcole!
Thus Bonaparte with bold self-assurance pointed to his

undeniable place in the honourable picture-gallery of French history, as the last figure in the row of those great men who have achieved deeds of heroism. But a Louis XVIII finds no place at Napoleon's side: "What will you do with a buried power? A strong current keeps its own path through the ocean waves."

*　　*　　*　　*　　*

Thus, in spite of great differences in antecedents and character, Bonaparte and Fouché were thrown into mutual relations by the force of circumstances. Neither of them wished to assign to the Bourbons a position at the head of France, both of them, therefore, felt their influence had its firmest foundation in the continuance of the work of the Revolution. Here Fouché's dark past, so fraught with dread responsibilities, united him in a mysterious way with Bonaparte's boundless self-sufficiency and ambition. Napoleon's Corsican birth and earlier military career had combined hitherto to keep him somewhat remote from the inner happenings of the French Revolution; so much the greater at first was his need of a Fouché, that "roué" of the Revolution, to quote Talleyrand once more.

Chapter XIV

From the Brumaire Coup d'État
to the Permanent Consulate

FOUCHÉ's position was soon established during the early days of the Consulate. Working with Bonaparte, he endeavoured to reconcile the Royalists and Conservatives with the new rule. Amidst general approval a decree was passed in March 1800 that henceforth no Frenchmen should be branded as *émigrés* and thereby be made outlaws ; only those who had fled before December 25, 1799, were to incur this penalty. Their relatives were no longer to be held responsible for the *émigrés'* sayings and doings. A steady stream of applications reached Fouché from exiles who wished to return to their native land. On the whole he did his utmost to further their wishes, being glad of a chance to make friends even in the Royalist camp. Yet he never lost sight of his right as Minister of Police to keep those who returned under supervision. And should it prove impracticable to advance their cause, he liked to shelter himself behind the dreaded Bonaparte—as in the case of a prominent *émigré*, Casimir de Guiche. The Royalist disturbances, that up till then had been active at the mouth of the Loire, in Brittany and Normandy, were quelled by conciliatory measures as well as by force, and in the early spring of 1800 general peace was reached along this front. Numbers of the enemy, " the Chouans ", streamed to Paris to enjoy themselves, to get a sight of the new conditions and to meet old acquaintances.

Meantime, of course, Fouché did not forget to show like favour to his former friends, the Jacobins. A number of them after the *Brumaire coup* had been condemned to deportation, but Fouché succeeded in preventing the sentence from being carried into effect, and, thanks to his efforts, their only penalty was to be kept under observation for the time being. Some former followers of the Socialist Babeuf who had been kept in prison since 1795 were set at liberty by Napoleon as the result of Fouché's intervention. Thus he formed personal ties in every direction. In his waiting-room a Royalist plotter, such as Bourmont, might be seen in peace and harmony with such a shady Jacobin go-between as Méhée. It was a continuation of the balance of power aimed at during the time of the Directory.

The course of events meantime developed quickly. The Royalists, whether in exile or at home, were alike grieved that Bonaparte did not follow Monk's example—the General who, after the great English Revolution of the seventeenth century, restored the lawful monarch to his throne. The new state of affairs seemed to offer, however, one advantage, viz. that there was now only one ruler to be dealt with. If he were got rid of, everything no doubt would revert to the expectant Louis XVIII. The latter's brother, the Duke of Artois, then planned a *coup* from England by means of his secret emissaries in Paris, Hyde de Neuville and his confidants. Bonaparte was to be killed or kidnapped as he was on his way from Paris to his country palace of Malmaison. But in May 1800 Fouché had found out this proposition, "the English Agency", as it was called. Those implicated were arrested, sent up for punishment and their papers confiscated.

The Royalists appeared in an ugly and unexpected light. But Fouché triumphed, was admired for smartness and overwhelmed with praise by Napoleon. The latter had, moreover, just then special reasons for wishing to be on friendly terms with a Minister of Police who had influence amongst those of every party. The war of 1799 was still going on against the Austrians, and Bonaparte was just thinking of starting for Italy to venture on a decisive trial of strength with them. His whole position depended upon its issue. If he was killed or even suffered a reverse only, much might depend on Fouché's course of action in Paris.

On June 20, 1800, two couriers arrived in the capital bringing news that the French army had been defeated by the Austrians at Marengo and was now retreating. It is impossible to describe the perplexity that reigned in the Government circles. Bonaparte's brothers, Joseph and Lucien, each dreamt of rising to power on behalf of the family. Many of the Left party flocked round Carnot, formerly a member of the Committee of Public Welfare and now Minister of War. Fouché, too, was pointed out as the hero of the hour, although he seems, as a matter of fact, to have assumed an attitude of suspicion whilst he coolly awaited events. Next day there came, too, the relief of the news that Bonaparte had won the victory at last.

*　　*　　*　　*　　*

The unstable balance of power in France, however, could not continue in face of this sudden increase in the First Consul's prestige. The triumph at Marengo resulted in quite new developments. Bonaparte's ambition, which, according to his own statement, always increased with the onward march of events, rose to great heights before the growing storm of applause which met him everywhere on his return at the beginning of July to France and Paris. His opinion is reflected in his words to a confidant in August 1800 : "I am convinced that no one but myself, neither Louis XVIII nor Louis XIV, at this moment would be able to rule France. If I disappeared, it would be a calamity." Such utterances showed that his new course henceforward was to be towards absolute power without the slightest regard for Bourbon gnashing of teeth or Jacobin protests.

Bonaparte thought he had definitely settled the Bourbons, whose chief hope had lain in the help of the foreign Powers, by his military success, which, moreover, had made England incline to peace. He now directed his ill-will mainly against the Jacobins, those theorists with their impractical ideas that could only cause confusion in a well-ordered State. Carnot, compromised, moreover, by his behaviour during the Marengo days, was soon compelled to leave his post as Minister of War. Neither had regicide Fouché, the man from Lyons, a much firmer hold on the First Consul's favour just now. Behind Napoleon there were now a group of men—headed by Lucien Bonaparte, the Consulate's Minister of Internal Affairs who were eagerly urging an attack on the work of the Revolution. The *émigrés* ought to be brought back in the greatest numbers possible to France, where they would soon settle down comfortably under Bonaparte's strong rule ;

Catholicism must again take a prominent position in the country in open union with Rome. Last, but not least, Bonaparte must be made permanent ruler for life and the succession be secured to his family.

Fouché put a good face on a bad business, and the more the former *émigrés* were honoured, the more he tried to get into intimate relations with them. A depraved and mercenary deserter from their ranks, bearing the historic name of Montmorency-Luxembourg, served as Fouché's tool in these efforts of his. Thus Fouché came into personal touch with his worst and most artful enemy amongst the old Royalists, Bourmont, who in the future was to be known not only as a deserter from Napoleon to Louis XVIII immediately before the battle of Waterloo, but also, by his expedition to Algiers in 1830, as the founder of French colonial rule in North Africa. Fouché has been accused of suspecting Bourmont unjustly of plots against the France of Napoleon's days, but the Minister of Police probably had several reasons for his opinion even if it did not prove quite accurate. Now, Fouché is supposed, in a private interview with Bourmont, to have expressed himself with amazing frankness : " Take the leadership of all the Royalists. Leave out some for me in order to make the others more secure, and I will help you to increase your weight with them all. I still have great influence over the pronounced Republicans, and if you join me we can control as we like the fortunes of the State, since we rule the two parties that comprise amongst their members all men of any spirit. We have as our opponents only those blockheads of Moderates, but you know, of course, that they are cowards who are not

126

much to be feared." If Fouché really did speak in this way, it was doubtless an attempt to entice Bourmont to let out party secrets. It is not to be wondered at if the latter in terror repelled all such impudent propositions. Yet when, on September 23, 1800, some Chouans carried off the Senator Clément de Ris from his castle of Beauvais, in Touraine, in order to extort a ransom from his family afterwards, Fouché cleverly utilized his connection with this very Bourmont, who allowed himself to be persuaded that the Chouans, by their insolent deed, might bring ruin to all Royalists. Bourmont saw to it that Clément de Ris was set at liberty —an occurrence to which we shall come back in Chapter XVII.

The contest between the reactionaries and Fouché broke out in November 1800, when Lucien Bonaparte, as Minister of Internal Affairs, sent out to his subordinates throughout the country a pamphlet entitled, *A Comparison between Cæsar, Cromwell, Monk and Bonaparte*. In this publication he asserted that the First Consul ought to be made Dictator. He was worthy of such a position, since he was a representative of the educated and well-to-do, not of the uncivilized masses. This was springing a mine prematurely, for public opinion was not yet ready for such a strong dose of the new monarchical doctrines. Fouché, as usual, seized his opportunity, in his reports cleverly pointed out the danger of the situation to the First Consul, who started back in consternation, and the Police Minister's victory was won. The pamphlet was confiscated everywhere, and Lucien Bonaparte, in spite of his fury, was compelled to give up his post as Minister of Internal Affairs.

But Fouché, after this, was a thousand times more closely watched by his opponents. They were much annoyed over his vigorous supervision of the Chouans, and delighted when, in November, discovery was made of a Jacobin plot against Bonaparte's life quite possibly caused to a certain degree by their own insidious proceedings. The situation suddenly became acute when quite unexpectedly a frightful attempt was made on the life of the First Consul when on his way to the Opera. An "infernal machine", two barrels of gunpowder loaded on to a cart, exploded in Rue Nicaise, killing twenty-two persons and wounding twenty-six more, although Bonaparte, by a mere chance, escaped unhurt. The excitement was unprecedented. Why had not the Minister of Police prevented this deed ? Without the slightest doubt on account of his criminal consideration for those arch-disturbers of the peace, the Jacobins, those men of "filth and blood", to use Bonaparte's expression. The First Consul was hailed as the only one who could deliver the country from these offscourings. Lucien Bonaparte and his followers rejoiced, for they hoped that the disaster would cast its shadow over the Jacobins' ideal, the Republic, and thus prepare the way for a strong monarchical constitution.

Fouché hastily took in his political sails. Bonaparte's private secretary, Bourrienne, whose memoirs on other occasions are not always to be relied on, seems trustworthy when he says : " The cleverest actor would not be able to reproduce his calm demeanour under Bonaparte's outburst of wrath, his reserve, his patience under accusations, all the protests that lay in his silence, and above all in his broken hints." It is said with

128

DANTON

From a print in the Carnavalet Museum

more or less foundation that this derisive attitude of Fouché's irritated his antagonist exceedingly. " Why don't you speak ? " he was asked. " Let them chatter ", was the reply. " I will not compromise the safety of the State. I will speak when the right time comes. He laughs best who laughs last." It was the Royalists who, according to Fouché's fixed opinion, had been guilty of the attempt.

Fouché's position, however, weakened before the storm of reactionary opinion. To subdue the unrest and to gain time for his police inquiries he did not hesitate to make a sacrifice. He stooped so far as to draw up a list of one hundred and thirty persons who ought to be deported—old terrorists who were now to expiate their sins of the years from 1792 to 1795. The list was compiled at random, and, as Fouché said, certainly not all these unlucky men had been seized with a dagger in their hands, but they were, at any rate, all capable of sharpening it. A resolution of the Senate on January 5, 1801, confirmed Fouché's proposal. Many of those thus deported never saw France again. Cool audacity and stubborn lust of power are seen closely allied on this occasion in the attitude of the former Convention Representative. But would it ultimately have been better for the revolutionary party and their aims if Fouché had been deposed as Minister of Police in favour of some tool of the reactionaries ?

Soon came Fouché's hour, the greatest in his dramatic life. On January 9 the police arrested a Royalist, Carbon, who confessed to having driven the powder-cart at the attempt on Napoleon's life. His accomplices and comrades were soon crowded into the prisons, where the authorities even lodged the Royalist leader, Bourmont, the very man who so lately had hoped to replace Fouché as Minister of Police. Death sentences followed in great numbers. But in spite of all, the resolution to deport the one hundred and thirty Jacobins still held good. It was Bonaparte's policy always to steer his course to the Right.

Inch by inch Fouché meantime still tried to put up a defence against the superior power. He had certainly shown active co-operation in securing the return to France in the autumn of 1800 of a large number of persons, amongst others, *émigrés'* wives and children, and those who had been exiled on suspicion alone, as well as priests who, without more ado, had been driven in crowds over the frontier during the Terror—in all 52,000 of the 145,000 *émigrés*. Fouché persistently insisted that careful distinction must be made between the different groups of exiles who had been compelled to leave the country for different reasons—on one hand, those who had evaded compliance with the revolutionary laws, on the other, those who had fought against the Republic. Those who were returning must also be kept under careful and individual supervision, each in his own town. But Bonaparte wished to take rapid strides in gaining the Royalists' favour. In April 1802 a decree was also issued providing for a general amnesty, the only exceptions being those who had led armed attacks against France, former officers in hostile armies, or Bourbon courtiers. Only a couple of thousand persons then remained in the *émigré* lists. It was no longer possible to exercise any real supervision over the returned Royalists. The decree was the more perilous since the home-comers were grumbling at not receiving any compensation for their property confiscated during the Revolution, and only a few considered they were bound by the promise of loyalty which they had to take *en masse*.

Fouché fought as eagerly and with equal want of success against the incipient religious reaction. Immediately after *Brumaire* he had published a circular letter to the " constitutional " bishops, leaders of the State-protected National Church founded by the Revolution, calling upon them to train their people to obedience to the Republican laws. This was a distant echo of Fouché's former rule in Nevers. He added that the bishops had, of course, the comfort of seeing religion in France brought back to what had always been a restorative for failing forces, viz. to the very foundations of its constitution. Perhaps Fouché then remembered his enthusiasm as an Oratorian for the purity and equality of the earliest Christian Church. In any case, he continued to hope that France would be spared from the superstitious influence of the popish rule, which might so easily be placed at the Royalist service. Fouché, however, noticed, soon after the battle of Marengo, that dangers were arising from this quarter, too, for the men and memories of the Revolution. Bonaparte, with a statesman's keen insight, saw that the majority of the nation, in spite of everything, still continued to show leanings to Catholicism, and he boldly attempted to come to an understanding with Rome so that, in alliance with the Pope, he might be able the more effectually to rule men's minds in France. Against such a development the French National Church resisted to the very utmost, and through the agency of Bishop Périer, in Clermont, Fouché fanned the flames of opposition with all his might. The Papal Nuncio, Spina, wrote home to Rome : " The Minister of Police makes me tremble." Bonaparte certainly got the upper hand at last, but when a new Church agreement, the *Concordat*, was introduced in the spring of 1802, in accordance with his views, and all the bishoprics were filled by fresh Church dignitaries, Fouché was successful in securing the appointment of several of his friends. Périer again assumed his office in Clermont, Pancemont in Vannes. Abbé Belloy became Archbishop in Paris in place of a priest with popish leanings. These were concessions that proved that the field had not yet been entirely surrendered to the forces of reaction.

* * * * *

Bonaparte, as champion for peace abroad and order at home, for mercy to the *émigrés* and respect for the Catholic Church, shone as a bright and burning light in the eyes of the majority in city and country alike. But in the shadow of his splendour there moved an indignant crowd, his former companions in the revolutionary army, who, worried by their inactivity, were angry at the restraint of the peaceful conditions and cursed the influence that *émigrés* and priests seemed all at once to be getting in the revolutionary Republic of earlier days. When during the Easter feast, 1802, the completion of the Concordat was celebrated in the Church of Notre-Dame in Paris with an impressive service in the old Catholic style, Bonaparte, at its close, asked one of his Generals, Delmas, how he had liked the ceremony.

" All that was missing was a million men who have
laid down their lives to destroy what you are building
up ", was the frank answer. The former revolutionary
soldiers looked with scornful gestures at Bonaparte's
alliance with the Pope—somewhat as Fouché and his
partisans had, on one occasion, smiled maliciously at
Robespierre as the high-priest of " the Supreme Being ".

It is quite certain that Fouché shared, heart and soul,
in the bitter feeling amongst the officers who, like the
constitutional priesthood, were his secret allies against
reaction. He had, moreover, his own special reasons
for not offending the army authorities, for who knew
when Bonaparte might be struck down by a dagger-
thrust or musket-shot? Then the Republic might
again need a sword at its head as before *Brumaire*. In
the ranks of the malcontents there already loomed the
figure of Bonaparte's heir—General Bernadotte, who, as
Minister of War in the summer of 1799, had organized
the defence of France, but who had been dismissed, and
afterwards had to watch his comrades reaping the harvest
which he had sown. Bernadotte, it is true, took good
care not to advocate any violent opposition to Bonaparte,
from whose wrath he was protected through his connection by marriage with Napoleon's brother Joseph,
but these facts only tended to increase the weight of the
cutting personal attacks that Bernadotte used to make
upon the First Consul in *salons* and at the officers' mess.

The outspoken Delmas and two blustering comrades were sent to prison in May 1803 for their
threat, when hobnobbing with their friends, to shoot
Napoleon. Fouché covered up the whole business in
silence, nor did Bonaparte wish it to be known that

there was any disaffection in the army. It was, however, more difficult not to give the alarm during the following month, when a real conspiracy came to light in Rennes amongst the body of troops under the command of Bernadotte himself. Two printed proclamations had been issued to both officers and men. " Soldiers, you have no longer any fatherland", was one of the statements it contained. "The Republic no longer exists, and your honour is stained." It was the old doctrine of strife between a twofold France—one revolutionary, the other reactionary—which had been revived again in spite of Bonaparte's attempt at reconciliation. As usual, of course, nothing could be proved against Bernadotte himself, but his Chief-of-Staff and several officers were thrown into prison. Bonaparte even now still shrank from bringing the matter into court, and was satisfied with dispersing the other 'discontented officers to distant commands. Meantime he strongly suspected Fouché of having fanned the flame of disaffection.

*   *   *   *   *

In March 1802 Bonaparte put the crowning touch to his work when peace was proclaimed with England. In the beginning of May the supporters of the First Consul in the Senate proposed that as a reward he should be invested with the Consulship for life. But Fouché fought to the utmost against the popular opinion. Why should a permanent dictatorship be set up just when strife and unrest had ended? That meant converting Bonaparte quite unnecessarily into a target for all the slings and arrows of adverse criticism from Royalists and Republicans alike, a target that might possibly give way under the attack. If national opinion was turned in this way to absolute rule, the Bourbons would find it easy to seize the power, if Bonaparte should die. Fouché himself, it is true, was not one of the Senators, but he knew secret methods of getting a hearing amongst their circles, and succeeded in persuading several of them that Bonaparte really only wished his Consulate to be extended for another ten years. This was also recommended by the Senate, to Bonaparte's annoyance.

Bonaparte was thus compelled to trust to other means for the attainment of his aim. A national vote was arranged, which at last granted him his desire of an hereditary position of power, and thus carried out the reactionary programme. The circle seemed to be complete, for the year 1802 clearly marked the restoration of an absolute rule, which in 1789 had been curtailed by the Friends of Liberty. The former class distinctions, too, found their equivalents in the social system bound up with the institution of the Legion of Honour and the notability assemblies of well-to-do and prominent men which were established throughout the country. But the Tribunal and Legislative Body, which, by the constitution of 1799, were to balance the Consular power, were despised and set at defiance by Bonaparte.

The state of general calm, which Fouché had so greatly helped to bring about, and which, in his opinion, made Bonaparte's dictatorship unnecessary, in a short time proved disastrous for himself. " The nigger has done his work, the nigger can go." Indeed, the very office that Fouché had filled had also been compromised by his stubborn and underhand opposition to Bonaparte's policy. In August 1802, therefore, the post of Minister of Police was abolished and its activities transferred to the authority of the Minister of Justice, " the Lord Chief Justice ". The contest was at an end—for the immediate present. Fouché could once again devote himself entirely to his own private affairs—as before the September of 1798.

Chapter XV

The Reign of Terror and the Empire

THE task of reconciling Catholics and returning *émigrés* with the rule of Bonaparte, the Corsican soldier of fortune, was of too delicate a nature for the First Consul to dare to sever all friendly relations with the ranks of the Left. Even fallen Fouché was, for the same reason, a power to be reckoned with, all the more since Bonaparte saw in him the very embodiment of the revolutionary principles. So when the post of Minister of Police was done away with, Bonaparte told Fouché that his brothers Joseph and Lucien had been instrumental in its suppression. And when Fouché, at his formal leave-taking, handed over to the First Consul the funds of the Ministry of Police, 2,400,000 francs, he received a full half of the sum total, a princely gift indeed. It was, moreover, accompanied by a flattering request that Fouché would still continue in the future to give Bonaparte the assistance of his good advice. Fouché was also nominated a member of the Senate, the authority on which Bonaparte relied more and more for the exercise of his power. When, in January 1803, the *sénatoreries* were formed, groups of crown-lands whose rentals went to favoured senators, Fouché received that of Aix, with a yearly rent list of twenty to twenty-five thousand pounds. Beyond all else, it was noticed that Bonaparte in connection with Fouché's nomination as Senator expressly praised his talents, power and loyalty in the exercise of

his duties as Minister of Police, and declared that should
the office ever be reconstituted, no one's claims could be
considered before his. This meant not only binding
Fouché to Napoleon, but directly calling upon him to
continue taking a part in politics. Fouché also desisted
from further contest with the First Consul and his
party. Just as during the period from 1795 to 1798 he
had been the Director Barras's secret spy amongst
parties and individuals, so now he at once put his
intelligence system at the service of Bonaparte, who
soon received from Fouché secret police reports more
exact and far-reaching than those dispatched to him
by his Minister of Justice, Régnier. The latter suspected that Fouché still had friends both in the higher
and lower police offices, and was anxious to clear out
all old Jacobins from his staff of subordinates; his
intention, however, to his amazement, was frustrated
by the opposition of the First Consul. Bonaparte was
still less able to quarrel with Fouché as the war with
England began again in May 1803. Earlier in the spring
Louis XVIII, as we have already mentioned, rejected
Bonaparte's gesture of reconciliation. Storm-clouds
were gathering round his power.

* * * * *

The Bourbons and their adherents now formed a
poor and unimposing company, treated with contempt
by England, Russia and Prussia, and split up into the
respective supporters of Louis XVIII, his brother, the
Count of Artois, and their friend the Duke of Orléans.
But there was living in London a Chouan, who, in his
own person alone, was an opponent more to be dreaded

than the whole company of *émigrés*, Georges Cadoudal, the son of a Breton peasant. Deeply involved in the previous civil war, he was irrevocably bound to the Royalist cause; owing to the threats of his own partisans, he had in 1800 given up all attempts at reconciliation with Napoleon. Then—so the report goes—he said to a friend : " If ever the King should come to the throne, he would do well to shoot us. You and I will never be anything but conspirators." Behind the back of the other *émigrés* this desperate man entered into league with the English Government, received a million francs, and was then taken over to France. In August 1803 Cadoudal appeared in Paris without Régnier's police having any inkling of the matter. He hoped to be able to collect from Brittany a company of at least two hundred reckless fellows for the capital, and at the head of these to make an open attack upon Bonaparte and either kidnap or kill him. Simultaneously with this attempt, one of the French princes was to be prevailed upon to raise the standard of rebellion on the coast. Cadoudal, however, waited in vain for his followers, and he would not stoop to a simple assassination of Bonaparte. Thus the autumn of 1803 passed by.

At this period there was living in London General Pichegru, a soldier of renown, and a man of defiant personality, who in 1797 had been deported to Guiana for Royalist riots, but the next year had escaped to England. Pichegru was a sworn enemy of Bonaparte's absolute rule. He was visited quite unexpectedly by a French General, Lajolais, who in the midst of the war had secretly crossed the Channel. Lajolais had once served as Chief-of-Staff with Pichegru's former companion-in-arms, Moreau, the first soldier in France next to Bonaparte. Pichegru was now pleased to hear that Moreau too was up in arms against Bonaparte, who had hushed up the report of Moreau's victories and deprived him of honour and glory. The real fact was, however, that Moreau, a modest man by nature, had been incited against the First Consul by his wife and his mother-in-law, the intriguing Mme Hulot. Lajolais assured Pichegru that Moreau could be relied upon to over-throw Bonaparte and to restore the Bourbons to the throne! At this Pichegru beamed with delight, for, supported on one hand by Cadoudal and on the other by Moreau, it would be possible to unite Royalists and Jacobins in an attack on Bonaparte. Pichegru, in short, crossed over secretly in January 1804 and soon joined Cadoudal and his men in Paris, the police still having no idea of the danger. His interview with Moreau, however, turned out a disappointment, for the latter declared quite straightforwardly that he, it was true, did not care what happened to Bonaparte, but also that, as a Republican, he, under any conditions whatever, would take no part in reinstating the Monarchy. He would have nothing at all to do with Cadoudal. But neither did he consider it consistent with honour or loyalty to denounce the conspirators to the authorities.

*   *   *   *   *

" The air is full of daggers ", Fouché wrote with justice in a report to Bonaparte, who was keenly alive to the danger and urged on the police to more active vigilance. Napoleon now himself intervened, if we may believe G. Lenotre, in a way which is particularly significant, and which shows that he can in no way be exonerated from personal participation in the violent methods used by the French police of that period. It was essential at any cost to discover the enemy, and on January 25, 1804, he gave an order that five Royalists, in prison on suspicion of complicity in plots, should without further ado be brought before a court martial, condemned to death and shot ; by this process possibly one of them might be induced to open his lips. That was, as is evident, a method of administering justice that recalls to our minds the Moscow of 1927. Over and above this, one of the unfortunate men, Querelle by name, was scarcely implicated at all, but had been selected on the ground that he was known to be a coward. Querelle, therefore, had to stand near and watch how two of his companions in misfortune were brought to the place of execution, and then look on as the platoon of soldiers were drawn up to escort him too to death. It was too much for his weak nerves, and, seized by uncontrollable panic and quite beside himself, he revealed all that he knew. Cadoudal had been in the city for several months !

Bonaparte was furious. One of Régnier's colleagues, Réal, assisted at the police investigation. This meant stretching out a finger to Fouché, for Réal was his confidant. On February 14 the panic increased, for, early in the morning, the police at the last moment prevented a prisoner, the Royalist officer Bouvet de Lozier, from hanging himself. " Still under the shadow of death ", with bloodshot eyes and blood-stained face, Bouvet now confessed everything—as we are told by Desmarest, chief of the secret police, in his memoirs.

141

Pichegru, too, was in Paris, and Moreau taking part in schemes for an attempt on Bonaparte's life! On the same day a special consultation was held before Napoleon, at which Fouché was also present and advised careful deliberation.

Moreau was arrested and a special court instituted to try his case. It was almost like a state of siege in Paris whilst search was being made for the other conspirators. " Fetch Fouché," was Bonaparte's nervous command to Réal on one occasion at the beginning of March. Fouché, however, seems to have preferred to await natural developments. The prisons were filled with prisoners who were tortured, it is said, to extort confessions. At last Cadoudal and Pichegru both fell into the hands of the police. The latter was found one morning in his cell strangled, either by his own hands or by Napoleon's orders. The First Consul was beside himself. He noticed that his political opponents in France were enraged at Moreau's fate, and said that he had been arrested without reason and from personal motives of revenge. This suspicion was confirmed when, in the early summer, Moreau was sentenced to only two months' imprisonment, and in the end was pardoned by the Emperor Napoleon, but banished. But Cadoudal, with a smile of bravado, wended his way to death at the head of most of the remaining conspirators.

*　　*　　*　　*　　*

Bonaparte's dreams of a rapturous and united France under his sceptre were dissipated as if by magic. He thought he saw through the English Government's insidious intention of promoting at any cost a movement in France in favour of compliance and peace. Had not Pitt said to Bonaparte's Ambassador, Otto : " What importance can be attached to a Government that depends on a pistol-shot ? " These words had also become the slogan in the Chouans' secret schemes. The Bourbons, whom Bonaparte had lately despised, appeared, in the lightning-flash of the moment, likely to be in the future a more reliable power than that which he was trying to establish with the help of well-disciplined bayonets. Louis XVIII's declaration of the secret power of history over the present was exemplified in the dangers threatening the First Consul on every side. When would revolutions cease in this torn and tortured France ? Fear, the faithful attendant of the idea of annihilation through these agitating times, also perhaps dropped its poison into the brimming cup. But it was not the habit of a Napoleon Bonaparte to moan and suffer, but rather to hack his way out of jungle and thicket.

In the early days of March 1804 news reached Bonaparte that one of the French Princes, the Duc d'Enghien, was preparing in Ettenheim in Baden to begin a regular campaign on to the French side of the frontier. One of the exiled revolutionary Generals, Dumouriez, was with him. Bonaparte lost his self-command. On March 10 he held a special council with his advisers, Fouché amongst them, and decided—only the Consul Cambacérès giving an adverse vote—to seize the Prince. His order was carried out, but when Enghien's papers were confiscated, it was clear that the report of his schemes was false, that not Dumouriez, but the old harmless Marquis de Thumery was living with him, and that he had never had anything to do with Cadoudal and his designs.

Bonaparte, however, was no longer to be restrained. Those who declared him an outlaw should at least feel the effects of his unlimited power! A court martial was appointed with definite instructions, and met at eleven o'clock in the evening of March 20. The Prince's request for an interview with Bonaparte was refused. He was straightway sentenced to death for his plots against France, and at half-past two the next morning was shot in the castle moat of Vincennes.

Was Fouché, who had advised Enghien's arrest, also an accomplice in his death? Such a rash and violent proceeding was undoubtedly not to his taste. On the contrary, there is great reason to think that his opinion in the matter is accurately expressed in the following utterances ascribed—rightly or wrongly—to him: "This is worse than a crime, it is a blunder", and, "This is a shot fired unnecessarily." But the act in the castle moat of Vincennes was a turning-point in Fouché's life as well, by its profound effect on Bonaparte's fate. Henri Welschinger, who in two celebrated works has depicted the Duc d'Enghien's unblemished life and tragic death, has pointed out that Bonaparte at the end of 1803 intended to go the whole length and assume the position of absolute monarch of France, but that he was afraid the former revolutionaries would think that, in taking the step, he was secretly acting on behalf of the Bourbons. Perhaps in the same way there was a touch of calculated design in his action against the Duc d'Enghien. In any case Bonaparte by this deed broke for ever with the *ancien régime* and its dynasty,

144

and compelled each and all to choose between him and the Bourbons. Of Coulaincourt, one of the members of the court martial, Bonaparte said to Josephine : "He is compromised. That is no great harm. He will serve the better for it."

Welschinger also repeats the reply that Bonaparte gave to the former regicide, Cambacérès, when he objected, on March 10, to Enghien's arrest : "You have grown very stingy with the Bourbon blood." Just as Robespierre and his friends in their time would not grant the deposed monarch any earthly existence in their citizen Republic, so Bonaparte attempted in his fury to destroy entirely the royal house that might dispute his place as head of the Kingdom of France. The Revolutionists' enthusiastic worship of the supreme power of the people had, it is true, been replaced in the Government of France by the Corsican's overpowering confidence in his own personal strength, but both were alike in the relentless defiance of, and their opposition to, the past history of France and to those tragic figures who upheld its cause.

*   *   *   *   *

In this blood-stained soil Napoleon Bonaparte's empire was installed as the heir to the crimes of the Revolution, but for that very reason also a protection for its work and workers. Indicative of this is the fact that Fouché himself was one of the most eager in his efforts to establish the Empire. After the happening of 1802, Bonaparte's power, of course, was in reality absolute. What did it matter to such as Fouché if the symbols of the Republic were exchanged for the imperial emblems on the banner of France? But Bonaparte had now vanquished the Bourbons once for all, and even the Royalists, who before had been inclined to support his cause, drew back in consternation at his course of violence. Consequently it was Fouché who, in the Senate's Committee, took the initiative concerning the change in Constitution. So it came about that when the Senate, on March 27, congratulated Bonaparte on his escape from the attempt on his life, it also exhorted him "to complete his work by making it immortal". Even those who before had furthered reaction, now shrank from giving Bonaparte unlimited power, but Fouché had no such scruples. In Bonaparte's Privy Council he insisted that no hampering restrictions must be imposed upon the Emperor in the new Constitution. The guarantees that Fouché needed already existed in the very nature of the conditions after the murder of the Duc d'Enghien.

After the Empire was established by a decree of the Senate on May 18, 1804, it was not long before Fouché again rose to honour, power and splendour. Josephine, who at Napoleon's side took the foremost place in the State, continually needed Fouché's help against her husband's relations and used her influence on his behalf with the Emperor. In their fear of Napoleon even the Royalists who were living in France hoped that Fouché would again become Minister of Police, and as such somewhat quell his master's outbursts of rage. In addition to this, Napoleon, after the events of the spring, was dissatisfied with the police system. "Fouché would not have landed me in this quandary", he is reported to have said with special reference to the management of the Moreau affair. Since Enghien's death and the institution of the Empire were looked upon as a challenge to Russia, Prussia and Austria, a fresh European war might be anticipated, whilst England was a continual source of anxiety on the French coasts. Fouché's opponents also agreed that under such conditions he was the only man capable of successfully accomplishing the difficult task of maintaining internal order. When the Emperor still hesitated, Fouché took the initiative himself in a letter to Joseph Bonaparte, in which, amongst other things, he said : " I wish for the first place not in the Empire, but amid the dangers to which the Emperor may be exposed and amongst the conspiracies which will threaten the dynasty that we have just established."

In July 1804 Fouché was at last appointed once again as the French nation's Minister of Police.

Chapter XVI

Minister of Police

" IF he could, he would do the cooking for the whole world ", was the character given to Fouché by Savary, his successor as Minister of Police, an allusion to the extensive, secret and ambiguous nature of Fouché's activity. His police, too, became a terror to all opponents of the ruling authority. " A monster brought forth in the revolutionary pond by the mating of anarchy and despotism ", was the designation given to him by René de Chateaubriand, whose brother was entrapped in Fouché's net. An expert in the underground activity of that period, such as Talleyrand, observed in his contemptuous way that a Minister of Police of Fouché's style was " a man who must have a finger in everything that concerns him and, above all, in what is no concern of his ". Another of Fouché's opponents, the reactionary Fiévée, dwells especially on the fact that he favoured the Jacobins at the expense of the Royalists, and declares that whilst police are " an institution for the prevention of dangers to the State ", Fouché's police are " an institution for the prevention of dangers to which the old revolutionary spirit might be exposed ". In essence, if not in form, Fouché's own definition is quite in agreement with the foregoing : " The Minister of Police has the charge of all branches of public order." That he did not even exclude Napoleon from his impertinent interest is clear

148

from his advice to his successor, Savary, to keep an eye on everything except himself. Fouché's intensive activity, however, was certainly not only an expression of his character, but also a profound necessity in the France of his day. The stability and morals of any community undoubtedly depend, to a high degree, on whether its inner development is allowed opportunity to continue in undisturbed quiet throughout all classes of society. Now the Revolution had brought with it a frightful upset in all social and economic relations. Soon, too, want began as well. No one knew what the morrow might bring. Politics encroached in a ruthless and incalculable fashion upon personal conditions that before, through hundreds of years, had been ruled by established custom. When, therefore, after the end of the Reign of Terror, even this elementary order broke down entirely in a number of places in the country, confusion reached its highest point. The Royalist riots were but one detail in the picture, for gangs of the homeless and impoverished were everywhere helping themselves to what they wanted. It was such a state of affairs that Fouché took in hand, founding a real agency of effective control, suppressing riot and robbery, and extending a protecting hand over the division of property which was a result of the revolutionary crises. A German writer, Hans von Hentig, believes that he can distinguish two different branches of Fouché's work : first, the political police, whose endeavour it was to maintain the ruling power, and secondly, the public-safety police, who aimed at the establishment of stable and quiet conditions throughout the country. The boundaries of these two divisions were certainly of a fluid nature, but Fouché's contributions to the latter work were, in any case, so important that they ought always to secure him a prominent place in French history, whatever may be thought of the methods he employed.

It cannot be sufficiently emphasized that Fouché was an organizer of extraordinary power. His greatness in this respect is due to his creative power, since he was at once the architect and master-builder of the administrative structure. It is certainly true that he seems to have copied many of the methods of police control under *l'ancien régime*, but this only places his own achievement in its correct historical perspective, without any loss to its practical geniality and striking importance. It was, in fact, an indispensable condition of Napoleon's triumphant career and quite as essential a factor in it as was ever the Emperor's genius as a military commander.

Fouché was Minister of Police on four different occasions, viz.: (1) July 21, 1799, to September 15, 1802; (2) July 10, 1804, to June 3, 1810; (3) March 21, 1815, to June 23, 1815; (4) July 7, 1815, to September 15, 1815. During incomparably the longest time of this activity Napoleon was his master. " Separate and rule ! " was Bonaparte's principle in government; consequently Fouché had to share his authority with the Minister of Justice in the control of the heads of the local administration, the Prefects, and with the Ecclesiastical Minister in any questions concerning the clergy. Within his own official district he had a competitor in the Police Prefect of Paris, Dubois, who was indirectly in touch with the Emperor through Napoleon's valet, Constant. In 1804, when the police organization was

completed, in addition to Fouché, a council was created
consisting of three—for a short time four—members
responsible for different geographical districts, namely,
Dubois for Paris, Réal for the important North and
Western departments, Pélet de la Lozère for the rest
of France and parts of Italy. The last-named official,
like Dubois, very soon was one of Fouché's enemies
in the ruling circles. In addition to all the above,
Fouché's police were by no means Napoleon's only
instrument of supervision. General Savary, as chief of
the Emperor's military guard, and General Moncey,
as head of the *gendarmerie*—neither of them with any
liking for the Minister of Police—each had a staff of
agents and spies, who kept a watchful eye on Fouché's
mode of procedure. Moreover, last but not least, there
came Napoleon's personal system of espionage, directed
to a certain extent against his own Minister of Police.

When Fouché, in spite of all these competitors,
became the most influential man in the country, next
to Napoleon himself, it was due to his fighting spirit,
which was but increased by opposition, critical situations and underhand traps, and also to his excellent
nervous system, at once sensitive and well hardened,
His chief weapon consisted of " bulletins ", his daily
reports to his master. The chief of the secret department
of the Ministry of Police, Desmarest, had, namely, to make
out, on the basis of the notices that poured in continually,
a detailed summary of the State affairs, and this summary
was afterwards scrutinized and corrected by Fouché.
From January 1809 to June 1810 this was supplemented
by a private notice in which the French leading circles
were passed in review with a sarcastic touch, from the

Empress Josephine down to the Police Prefect, Dubois. The bulletins were an effective means of influencing Napoleon's opinion, for they remained secrets between him and Fouché, and were sent on to the Emperor even when he was on a distant campaign. Fouché's privilege of always having access to Napoleon gave him additional means of parrying the thrusts that were aimed at him from every direction. A place was reserved for him, too, in the Emperor's Privy Council (*Conseil privé*) and in the committee dealing with ecclesiastical matters.

Of course we must not lose sight of the fact that the police system was really an organ for the Emperor's exercise of power and not Fouché's private property. If the latter view was often maintained at that period, it was doubtless a tribute to the Police Minister's power of making black white with the object of increasing the value of his political actions. Occasionally, as we shall see, the Minister of Police played the part of the intermediary who undertook to present a petition or a complaint in order, by such means, to win the favour of the public in his waiting-room, but afterwards he did not show any particular interest in his client's welfare. In Napoleon's eyes he thus appeared a trusted man, whilst Fouché could always point to the Emperor as the scapegoat for a refusal or any arbitrary display of power. Also, one of Fouché's well-wishers, Madame de Chastenay, complains in her memoirs that he did not have so much influence over Napoleon as he pretended.

In the execution of his office, Fouché understood quite as well as Napoleon the art of separating and ruling. Even his most highly placed colleagues, as a rule, only had details as their share in the more important political happenings, and were not able, on their own responsibility, to form any more vital decision, whilst Fouché jealously kept the ultimate control in his own hands. Yet he did not lack confidants. One such was Desmarest, a renegade priest, who, even in his new profession, displayed the father-confessor's psychological penetration and power " to try the heart and reins ". Fouché's adviser, Réal, a veteran from the days of the Terror, assisted him with his ability for inquisitorial methods, as agitating as they were violent. Nor were these methods of his any strangers to physical torture. The thumbscrew seems to have been a favourite means of loosening tongues. Certain police agents, such as the gigantic Pasques, appear to have extracted confessions by main force. Others, too, of his colleagues, like the absolutely unscrupulous Veyrat, abused their delicate task by blackmailing methods. Veyrat had thus a wonderful power of not noticing " wanted " persons if only they showed their gratitude to him in private by reasonable remuneration. Below the highest authorities there extended, step after step, a whole hierarchy of police agents and spies, permanent and temporary, public and private, men and women of different ranks of society, a personnel which we chance to know to a certain degree from lists drawn up by the Royalist contra-espionage. Certain money rewards were fixed for certain services, one hundred francs for information of a " wanted " Royalist or conspirator. " Such was the rate ", says d'Hauterive, " at which in those past days they assessed a man's liberty, at times his life even." The vast number of incoming notices were weeded out with transcendent skill. " A policeman ", said Fouché, " is like a diligence : he must start either cram-full or entirely empty of news." That being so, it was but natural that such news should be prepared in great quantity. With some exaggeration it is told that Fouché every day threw on one side, unread, two or three baskets of police reports. The whole apparatus was an expensive one, which in great measure was kept going on the rents of gambling-dens. Under the Empire the police estimates amounted to a yearly sum of three to four million francs. Napoleon complained with reason that he could not exercise any effective and detailed control over the expenditure of these funds.

Fouché ruled the country from Paris not only by Prefects in the various departments, but also by general Commissioners who were appointed in particularly disturbed areas. They specially worked in the large towns—clerical Lyons, Royalist Bordeaux and Boulogne, where Mengaud, that colleague of the Minister of Police, like a fierce dog kept watch over the forbidden coast traffic with England. The significant feature of this police system was that in its activities it rendered to a great extent the services required by both foreign and home politics. Pingaud, in his excellent study of Fouché and Napoleon, has pointed out that the former's dismissal from office in 1802 corresponds in time with the peace with England, his reappointment in 1804 with the beginning of a fresh period of war. The guarding of frontiers, so essential in times of unrest, was, as a matter of fact, in the hands of the police. Through their instrumentality, too, messages were conveyed from Napoleon to his vassal Kings. The police conducted a systematic espionage of the foreign diplo-

matists in Paris and had control of the passport system.
It supplied Napoleon with reports as to the state of
trade and industry during his great commercial feud
with England. Finally, it was Fouché's business to
bring back deserters. In the conquered territories he
had at different points, in addition to spies, public
deputies and general directors. The centre of the
northern intelligence system was Hamburg, where
Bourrienne collected and handed in reports, amongst
others, from hostile Sweden. Fouché, as Minister of
Police, had under his command quite a little coasting
squadron of guard-boats as well as the *gendarmerie* who
were told off for police service. Indeed, it sometimes
happened that certain military forces were placed at his
disposal in centres of disturbance, those so-called "flying
camps" that in 1806 and 1807, under General Boyer,
restored discipline in la Vendée, and in 1809, under
Colonel Henry, kept Normandy under law and order.

Fouché's jurisdiction also extended over the Press,
which he declared was responsible for the excesses of
the Revolution, and which, after the *Brumaire coup*, he
took in hand with great decision. Of seventy-three
newspapers he suppressed sixty at one stroke. The
evening before the publication of any newspaper it had
to be submitted to his scrutiny, and he also ordered a
weekly conference in the ministerial offices between the
editors and himself. Napoleon watched with jealous
care his activity in this direction, especially when a
determined peace propaganda began in the Press, in
opposition to the Emperor's desire. The censorship of
the theatres was also under Fouché's control. With truly
Russian bureaucracy he busied himself with suppressing

parts and crossing out repartees, even in one of Racine's masterpieces. The censorship of books, also under his control, was of a very similar nature. Attempts to revive unnecessarily any painful memories of the Revolution were sternly denounced. When Napoleon occasionally interfered in this work, his instructions might include a sarcastic reference at Fouché's expense, as, for example, when he remarked on May 22, 1805, that the title of *La Gazette de France* did not recall " any ugly memories of the Revolution ". Occasionally, it is true, Fouché indulged in somewhat ambiguous methods of influencing public opinion. When a manuscript describing the rebellion in la Vendée and containing bitter reflections on the writer's former companions-in-arms was found on a Royalist prisoner, Comte de Vauban, it was published at once, after the reflections had been made even more bitter, without the author's knowledge or consent.

Fouché's sphere of activity also included the control of the prisons. Immediately after *Brumaire* he enacted that every prisoner should make a written report of his case. In this way he also soon became master of this side of his work, in which he showed consummate discretion, mingled perhaps with a kind of fierce leniency. Apart from convicted criminals, prisoners were in confinement for the most diverse reasons. Some were locked up in accordance with the judge's pronouncement : " To be confined at Fouché's pleasure until the conclusion of peace " ; others were hidden away in this fashion so that their cases might not come into court, where they might be acquitted for want of proof. Imprisonment was inflicted in different degrees of severity, prisoners being condemned to the State prisons,

156

to imprisonment "with leniency", or to compulsory residence in some definite place. It was also a frequent occurrence that people were banished to a distance of from thirty to one hundred leagues from Paris. In this way circles of too ready talkers and plotters were broken up. The whole of this system is remarkable for its abnormal character of martial law. This was due in great measure to Fouché's unwillingness to allow disturbers opportunity of airing their views publicly during a trial and thus influencing public opinion for their cause.

Especially after the sensational trials in 1804 of Cadoudal and his fellow-culprits, the police, with Napoleon's approval, in certain cases, without further formalities, made away with "undesirables" to prevent their making any awkward disclosures at their trial. It has been said that this was justice in fact, though not in form, but in such procedure there is undoubtedly the possibility too of the "greatest justice" becoming only too often the "greatest injustice" instead. And the period which in the eyes of posterity has left to its honour a lasting monument of legislation in the *Code Napoléon*, has thus, in practice, provided an illustration of methods to be avoided in the administration of justice.

On the whole, it is plain that the results of these methods must directly depend on the personal character of the Minister of Police. Perhaps in this connection there may be truth in Madame de Staël's statement concerning Fouché, that, as a rule, he did not do more wrong than necessity required; perhaps in his heart of hearts he always remained the Terrorist of earlier days, with an indifference to human life and misery that only political considerations and calculations could veil and hide.

Chapter XVII

Fouché's Police at Work

It is Fouché's glory to have maintained internal order in France during the war-period from 1805 to 1810, in spite of the attempts to incite rebellion that were continually being made, especially by England, and in spite, too, of the wholesale conscriptions and the difficult economic crises resulting from these. Neither did the Royalists ever again succeed in working up any plots that could be compared with those in the eighteenth century.

The history of the Royalist movement from 1800 to 1810 deals instead partly with efforts to gain a secret influence over Napoleon, partly with a number of assassinations, acts of robbery and espionage, which certainly harassed him and his statesmen, but could scarcely have any appreciable effect upon the course of events as a whole. There were no longer any scenes like the incident during the campaign of 1793 in la Vendée, when Marceau, a Lieutenant in the revolutionary army, during a cavalry engagement, suddenly found himself face to face with the twenty-year-old la Rochejaquelein, the Captain of the la Vendée men, and both officers raised their swords simultaneously in a mutual salute. Instead, the outstanding dates in Fouché's feuds with the Chouans are—apart from the attempted murder of Bonaparte in December 1800—September 23, 1800, when a Senator, Clément de Ris, was carried off from his castle of Beauvais, in the Loire Valley, by four bandits, who endeavoured later on to utilize their captive as a hostage for an extortionate ransom ; also November 19 of the same year, when a former member of the Convention, Bishop Audrein of Quimper, was murdered, while on an official journey, by a band of Chouans ; and the night of July 23, 1806, when the Bishop of Vannes, Pancemont, was carried off by another company and kept as hostage until a sum of £24,000 in gold had been paid over to these highwaymen ; and lastly, June 7, 1807, when a band of highway robbers made off with a consignment of taxes of 60,000 francs. Thus the Chouans' outpost warfare in France for the royal cause had nothing in common with Roncevaux, where the sword was swung in knightly fashion to the faithless. These facts are disturbing, because they betray the kind of trade which the Chouans, the outposts on French soil of the lawful Monarchy and of England, were compelled to carry on to be able to get at their hated opponents and to pick up the poorest of livings for themselves. These dates with their sorry tales prove, too, how Fouché had succeeded in reducing and degrading his political enemies to nothing more than common evil-doers.

*   *   *   *   *

The first object of Fouché's endeavours was to keep in intimate and constant touch with the enemy. He no longer imagined, as in 1793, that Royalism was an evil spiritual power that must be destroyed at any cost, but saw in his opponents weak and faulty men of flesh and blood who must be rendered harmless in as painless and imperceptible a manner as possible. Taught by experience, Fouché had now adopted Robespierre's old principle, that the leader rather than the led ought to suffer for transgressions. This method, of course, destroyed the strength and continuity of the opposition which the enemy were trying to set up against Napoleon's and Fouché's power. The less notice attracted by police interference, the better. Nothing could more surely paralyse the spirit of rebellion than to let the malcontents see with horror one after another of their leaders disappear in silence and mystery.

The divining-rod with which Fouché went forward over his rough field of labour was originally put into his hands when the Chouans, after their temporary reconciliation with Bonaparte in the spring of 1800, swarmed out of their hiding-places and mixed, quite at their ease, with the other citizens of the Republic. Fouché, as usual, seized time by the forelock and let his intelligence-men conscientiously record every imaginable fact concerning the former foes, their personal appearance, habits, family life, associates and opinions. The reports that then came flooding in formed real and solid ground on which Fouché built later on, when internal peace came to an end and guerrilla war to the knife began once more between him and the Chouans. He now possessed information that enabled him to give every case its special treatment, and to avoid all provocative, unwise and summary action like that of 1793.

Practical as ever, Fouché summarized his varied knowledge of the offenders' world in two clearly arranged methods. He had made a veritable criminal

SAINT-JUST
From a print in the Carnavalet Museum

atlas—*topographie chouanique*—in which it was easy to find quickly the ports for which the Chouans generally made, the secret by-paths which they used on their journeys, the lodging-houses and taverns where they mostly put up, and the private houses where they were hospitably welcomed. Every fresh case added its quota to this interesting total. This atlas he supplemented by a complete offenders' album—*biographie chouanique*—containing descriptions of about one thousand persons as well as a complete list of the Royalist army outside the French frontiers. This was all a logical application of Fouché's opinion, " once a Chouan, always a Chouan "—*qui a chouanné, chouannera*—quite a modern point of view which is founded on a clear perception of the power of the past and the ineradicable tendency of the human will to move along the same old paths. In these records, too, we catch sight more clearly than elsewhere of Fouché's nature, his pedantic, exact and pedagogic character, in fact, the Oratorian who had turned Minister of Police. We are reminded, too, of Sainte-Beuve's description of a certain light of learning in the Oratorian order at the end of the seventeenth century, Sebastian Le Nain de Tillemont, who in the course of his historical and geographical studies put down all the names of persons and places in alphabetical order, thus laying the foundations of amazing scholarship. Perhaps Fouché in his criminal system did but follow in his own way a traditional method developed in the religious society to which he had once belonged.

In any case, this knowledge was no dead scholarship, as a couple of examples will show. After the attempt on Napoleon's life with the infernal machine the police stood for a moment nonplussed, without the slightest clue or suggestion. They gathered together the remains of the horse that had drawn the cart with the barrels of gunpowder and collected all farriers of the city to examine the horseshoes. One of them then found that he himself had, a little time before, shod the animal, and remembered that it had been led up by a man about five feet in height with a scar over the right eye. Fouché proved without difficulty that the description fitted a Chouan, who was also imprisoned after a time and found to be guilty of the crime. Another time it was reported that certain Royalist agents were not to be seen any longer in London, that away in Altona, where a number of *émigrés* lived, there were signs of glad expectation, and that, simultaneously with this, the beginnings of riot were noticed in la Vendée. The notices were methodically compared, and when counter-measures were quickly set afoot it was found they were by no means too soon. A well-known Chouan, Bertrand de Saint-Hubert, had been absent from his home for eighteen months. Then the report came in that his wife, known to be a virtuous woman, was pregnant. Inquiries were made in the district, and her husband was successfully tracked.

With increased intensity in police supervision we find a corresponding decrease in the harmony and *esprit de corps* amongst the Chouans. They tried to save their own skins by betraying their comrades to the authorities. Ernest Daudet, the historian of the Chouan feuds, tells in this connection the following curious tale: La Morlière, called the "ill-famed Caroline", formerly a Lieutenant in Louis XVI's Guards, offered

162

his services to the police to unmask the Royalists in Lyons, but his offer was rejected on account of his bad reputation, until at last an Abbé Rougier was arrested, on his advice. Then, when the abbé was being taken to Paris by a company of gendarmes, these were attacked by a crowd of masked men, who set Rougier at liberty. Several months later the officer in command of the gendarmes unexpectedly came across his former prisoner, and was going to arrest him again, but Rougier produced from his pocket a document from Dubois, the Prefect of Police in Paris, cancelling the original order for his arrest. He had now in his turn become a police agent. The man who had organized Rougier's rescue from the gendarmes was an old *émigré*, Roche, who, it is true, was rewarded for his exploit by the Royalists in the Lyons district with 12,000 francs, but was subsequently bitterly persecuted by the police. At last Roche lost heart, and giving himself up to the authorities, offered them his services against his former friends the Royalists. They accepted him gladly at first, but he soon proved a worthless tool, and they were pleased to let him disappear again over the frontier.

*   *   *   *   *

Fouché's method—mentioned already in Chapter XIV —of restoring the kidnapped Senator Clément de Ris to his home with the help of the Royalists themselves deserves some further elucidation. On this occasion Fouché very boldly offered freedom from punishment to those among the robbers who placed themselves under his personal protection. After the Senator had reached home safely, three of the worst bandits came therefore to the Minister of Police, who provided them with formal permits to live in Paris. These permits were, moreover, dated on the very day when the kidnapping had happened, and thus provided an alibi of the most convincing kind. Since all this course of procedure, if it had become known, would probably have seriously compromised Fouché, he continued to protect the three robbers from the hand of justice, even after he had otherwise completely broken in December 1800 with both Royalists and Chouans. But the remaining three kidnappers of Clément de Ris, who had not trusted themselves to Fouché, possessed, of course, no such guarantee of safety. Later on the Minister of Police also brought them to justice, and they ended on the scaffold.

The robbery of the tax-consignment that took place in Normandy in June 1807 gives us the clue to a puzzle in which love, sordid covetousness, loyalty to traditions and cruel treachery are to be found, not only mingled but almost inextricably entangled. We catch sight of strange figures in this wild confusion. In her castle of Tornebut the old Marquise de Cambray steadfastly awaits the arrival of her rightful lord and King, keeps His Majesty's rooms in the style befitting royalty, has his stables cleaned for the suitable reception of his horses and carriage, but also provides for a hiding-place in case dangers should lie in wait for the beloved monarch. Unfortunately the same simplicity of heart does not distinguish her daughter, the attractive Madame Aquet de Férolles, with her slender figure and dark beauty, who, divorced from her husband, enters into risky relations with the fiery Le Chevallier, a Chouan fanatic, who, without any scruples, involves his mistress in the attack on the tax-consignment. This proves the ruin of them all. Still another woman takes part in the dangerous game, the Marquise de Vaudabon, " a woman of medium height, not exactly beautiful, but very seductive, with her exceedingly fair skin, her languishing looks and her graceful bearing " (G. Lenotre). She is now in the middle thirties, a frivolous piece of goods, who long since has given up her longsuffering husband for other men, whom she chooses at first from among the Chouans. Driven by fear and a desire for money, she tries to get into touch with Fouché's police, and by her abandoned love of intrigue she becomes the evil spirit of the play, denounces one of Le Chevallier's comrades, Vicomte d'Aché, her former lover, to the police, and with malignant delight arranges the trap in which he is caught and done to death. Thus the Royalist enthusiasm is quenched in ignominy and blood ; the white-haired Marquise de Cambray is brought to the pillory, and her imprudent daughter expiates her crime under the blade of the guillotine. Another person figures in this connection, Licquet, the secretary to the Mayor of Rouen, a typical police official of the Fouché school. When the whole business looks dark and difficult to fathom he knows a plan. Under guise of sympathy with the hard fate of the captive Marquise de Cambray, he provides her in prison with a woman, who wins her confidence, carries her letters and reveals everything to Licquet, who goes so far as to have a forged document in the Vicomte's handwriting sent to her, to tell her of Louis XVIII's arrival in France. The old Marquise loses her self-possession, writes to the King, and thus provides Licquet with clear proof of her complicity. He entices Madame Aquet out of her safe hiding-place, and succeeds in cunningly rousing her anger against her mother, so that she confesses everything.

It is a gloomy picture in the annals of the police which is here revealed. The dark shadow of such deeds falls even upon Fouché. But it must not be forgotten that Napoleon gave a very bad example in similar methods. Thus, when they wanted to make de Rivière, a Royalist prisoner, speak, Napoleon wrote, on September 21, 1804, to Fouché that, with such an object in view, they might write and discreetly deliver to the captive a letter from the Duc d'Artois. The signature and seal need not be so very exact.

Meantime the two little daughters of Madame Aquet de Férolles were sent, accompanied by their aunt, on the far journey to the Emperor's camp in Austria to beg for their mother's pardon. They had waited a whole day on the steps of Schönbrunn Castle when Napoleon at last arrived and was stopped by the children's terrified prayer : " Give us back our mother ! " Napoleon inquired further into their errand, talked to his suite, and pronounced his decision : " That is not in my power." The little girls and their travelling companion continued their entreaties, but the Emperor was not to be moved from his purpose. Since the others implicated in the matter had suffered their punishment, it was impossible to exempt Madame Aquet, who had been more guilty than they.

The Emperor afterwards shared in Royalist eyes the responsibility for the prisoners' sad fate. But the

Minister of Police does not stand out in a very attractive light. We are suddenly reminded of the scene on the Brotteaux market-place in Lyons when the Convention Representative coldly surveyed through his glasses the destruction of the condemned by the platoon of gunners. But the comparison reveals no less the difference between 1793 and 1809. Then it was a question of wholesale action against unknown men, but now a case known to the Minister of Police in greatest detail.

* * * * *

In June 1808 two formidable Chouans were arrested. The one, Bouchard, fearing that he could not continue his flight, gave himself up to the gendarmes, and at the same time showed them where his companion Prijent was in hiding. Their hazardous life had destroyed all sense of honour in both the men. Prijent tried to obtain pardon by telling all that he knew of the Royalist arrangements and schemes, and many were arrested and executed as the result of this information. Amongst other things he told them of the colony of *émigrés* in Jersey, off the coast of Brittany, who kept a look-out on France, and there formed a centre for fomenting Royalist risings ; Prijent also proposed that he himself should go in Fouché's secret service to the island, keep a watch on the Royalist doings and listen to their schemes. But they considered Prijent too indiscreet and unreliable for such service. His companion, Bouchard, seemed to show greater qualifications for work of this kind. The plan was set in execution ; Bouchard got a good reception from the unsuspecting *émigrés*, and even succeeded in persuading

167

one of their leaders, Comte de Guyon, to make a trip over to France, where he was immediately arrested.

Imprudently enough Bouchard then returned to France, for the Emperor was now taking a personal interest in the affair. No doubt he had seen with satisfaction that the Chouans had been outwitted, but it was not his intention to allow Bouchard and Prijent to escape punishment on that account, and in October of the same year they were both executed by the Emperor's order. In this case there was no perversion of justice.

* * * * *

Thus Fouché's contest with the Chouans became underground warfare by means of mines and counter-mines, in which—so an author writes—" the principal thing in the men he appointed to fight the culprits was not moral but intellectual qualities ". The Minister of Police and his opponents alike pushed forward their outposts right into the enemy's headquarters, a situation which the former, of course, understood how to utilize to the utmost. Neither did he hesitate, when an opportunity offered, to pay the bandits in their own coin—murder and treachery. Thus, when the attempt with the infernal machine brought Fouché's entire position as Minister of Police into jeopardy, he proceeded to a remorseless attack on Georges Cadoudal, the conspirators' leader, who at the moment chanced to be in Brittany. Two renegade Chouans, Duchatellier and Becdelievre, were sent, one after another, to kill their former leader, either by force or poison. But Cadoudal, who was certainly not a man to be played

with, had them both done away with in the twinkling
of an eye.

"Where three are met together, I have always one
listening", Fouché is reported to have said; indeed,
he used to tell a joke about three individuals who had
been having a confidential talk, just between themselves, and who, each of them, came creeping up to
him afterwards to report what the others had said.
Those are tales in which his awestruck contemporaries
most fully believed. They lived in the conviction that
a web of watchful espionage was spun around back-
streets and taverns, hovels and market-places, theatres and
promenades, under this most skilful régime; probably,
on the whole, they were not far wrong. An aristocratic
lady, Madame d'Escars, in a moment of irritation,
tossed the bulletin concerning the battle at Austerlitz on
the fire in her boudoir—and suddenly found herself
sent off to the distant islands of Sainte-Marguerite. The
agents of the foreign diplomatists were bribed and gladly
opened their budgets in alliance with Fouché's agents.

Louis XVIII's cook in the English castle of Hartwell
was in the pay of Fouché, the man who would like "to
do the cooking for the whole world". In Paris the
crippled beggars at the street-corners listened in his
service to the public chatter. At a secret sign from a
passing police agent, they would suddenly start off on
the tracks of some undesirable figure who had to be
"shadowed". Fouché's spies sat in the cheapest seats
of the suburban theatres, fixing in their memories their
neighbours' unguarded words, just as they frequented
gambling-dens and inveigled secrets out of the excited
degenerates there. They did not forget either to creep

in amongst other listeners in the galleries of the police courts, where tongues are often set wagging by hate or sympathy. The spies themselves were frequently hopelessly at the mercy of the police, as the records of the police criminal registers faithfully showed, and possibly, too, their written acknowledgment that they had betrayed their old comrades in the sphere of crime. Whilst then these spies were trying to bring suspected individuals into the grip of the authorities, they were themselves inextricably snared in the widespread net of the police. Woe to the man who did not give complete satisfaction by his service! Hence the excellent working of the secret intelligence system.

Thus the echoes of " the public voice " were caught and reduplicated over and over again until they were forwarded on a larger scale to the Police Minister's ear-trumpet. Fouché, however, had a keen ear, trained to distinguish between an empty noise and the passionate notes of weighty import.

Personally, our worthy Minister of Police stands out as the obliging, understanding friend of all and sundry. With the same half-ironical, half-complaisant smile he listens in silence to the bitter-sweet (*aigre-doux*) conversation of the *émigrés* in the faubourg of St. Germain and to the bombastic bragging of the " new men " in their headquarters in the faubourg of St. Honoré. Now, as everyone knows, " he who keeps silence gives consent ", so the Minister of Police is a *persona grata* in many places. But meantime his brilliant brain is unceasingly busy, sifting and inspecting the flood of news and rumour that comes surging on through imperial Paris.

Chapter XVIII

The Empire and the Legacy of the Revolution

FOUCHÉ, with full consciousness of his purpose, looked upon the Empire as a safeguard of the work of the Revolution. After the scene in the Vincennes moat on March 21, 1804, he no longer needed to fear that Napoleon would capitulate to the Bourbons. Sometimes in his bulletins to the Emperor he would lightly touch on this memory, as when, mentioning the Royalists' custom of wearing mourning on January 21, the anniversary of Louis XVI's death, he hastened to add : " It is the same on the date of the Duc d'Enghien's death." Dangers still threatened, however. The powers of reaction still strove to leaven the Government from within, just as during the period from 1800 to 1802. It was therefore essential always to keep alive and strong the Jacobins' spirit as a power to be reckoned with. The Emperor still had no legitimate male heirs, and the succession must therefore be assured if the heritage of the Revolution was to be preserved intact. The constant wars which never ceased to threaten Napoleon's person and power must at last stop if the new order was not finally to collapse, and thus bring Fouché's whole political existence to utter ruin. For since the political excesses of the Directoire, he no longer believed in an actual re-establishment of the Republic.

It was these desires of his that were the mainspring of Fouché's line of action during his second period as

Minister of Police. We cannot therefore refuse to recognize him as a true statesman in this work of his, especially as it was carried out in the dusk of secrecy and uncertainty. Meantime Fouché had naturally to face the possibility that all his efforts might prove in vain. Anything common to humanity might, of course, strike down the Emperor. Then it would be essential to have at hand some power, bound to the revolutionary cause, strong enough to take up Napoleon's fallen mantle, or, at any rate, able to appreciate wise men's counsel. But Fouché, trained in the stern logic of the eighteenth century, liked to carry on his thoughts to their inevitable conclusion. If unfortunately all failed, if Napoleon's star set in the clouds and the sad hour should strike when the banner of the fleur-de-lis once more ruled the French nation—should he in such case throw down his tools in despair ? It was certain that the ideas of the Revolution had already been too deeply impressed in French history ever to be entirely forgotten again. Even a monarchic Government must probably show great consideration for the powerful interests created by its upheavals. It could not be denied that Fouché had " voted " and was one of those responsible for the crime of January 21, 1793. However, he no longer looked on the Bourbons and their following as steadfast guardians of monarchic principles, but as weak and erring men who might perhaps pay for his influential support even with the price of their willingness to forget the past. For the Bourbons must surely understand that there was now no chance of winning the game with but one colour in their hands.

* * * * *

Fouché therefore continued his earlier policy of protecting as far as possible the former revolutionaries from persecution, softening their lot and hushing up their follies with fatherly indulgence. His support was the more worth having since he ruled and managed everything quite independently for long periods during the Emperor's absence, viz. the autumns of 1805 and 1806, the spring of 1807, the spring, summer and late autumn of 1808, and from April to October, 1809. Every time Napoleon returned to Paris, he certainly overwhelmed his Minister with noisy reproofs for his wilfulness, but, as a witty authoress remarks in her memoirs, they were like a couple of lovers who are constantly returning one another's presents and letters, but cannot finally break off their engagement. Of the two, Fouché was undoubtedly the cooler and more calculating party, looking on ironically when Napoleon gave full vent to his feelings, sometimes playfully, but often too in real earnest. Robespierre, in his time, had been much more terrible in his significant silence. Later on, Pope Pius VII was credited with an answer to the Emperor's theatrical thunderstorms, " *Commediante! tragediante!* " which, whether historically true or not, probably quite correctly represents the mental criticism pronounced by Napoleon's hearers.

The hatred and jealousy lurking all around found expression, however, in a dangerous attack on Fouché in his very capacity of patron saint to the Jacobins. The Prefect of Police in Paris, the narrow-minded and splenetic Dubois, had long awaited his opportunity to pay out his superior officer; he could not bear the condescending smile with which Fouché would direct him to watch over "the young girls, the thieves and the lighting arrangements" in the capital. In June 1808 Dubois rejoiced that his dream had become reality, since he had, unaided, discovered a Jacobin conspiracy. Without informing Fouché, he hastened to communicate the matter to Napoleon, who was then in Spain, and to make several arrests.

The principal person in the affair was General Malet, a conspirator of a curious kind. His revolution patent was, namely, neither to kill nor to kidnap the Emperor, but simply to declare he was dead, and at the same time to publish a counterfeit decree of the Senate, appointing a new Government of reliable members of the Left party. The whole operation was thus to be performed by hypnotic suggestion; as in a dream the senators and generals were to dance for a few hours to Malet's piping. After that the whole thing would be an accomplished fact and the Republic brought back again. Emperor Napoleon would see himself degraded to a Corsican adventurer without hearth or home. Farcical as the very idea may appear, Malet had yet succeeded in winning over a few generals and some ex-members of the Convention to support his plan, which was soon rumoured far and wide. It seems then incomprehensible that Fouché should have no idea of what was proposed. Perhaps it was that he bided his time too calmly to act when the affair needed suppression, perhaps in his self-importance he underestimated its possibilities. On the other hand, it seems to be quite out of the question that Fouché should have built any treacherous schemes at all on such a fantastic creation as Malet's conspiracy.

In any case, Dubois' speedy interference in the matter came upon Fouché like a bolt from the blue. Napoleon's wrath rumbled from afar, as he congratulated Dubois on his discovery, reproached Fouché with a touch of suspicion in his tone for his slackness, and allowed the Police Minister's enemies in official circles to complete their inquiries. But Fouché preserved his unruffled calm, and both Réal and Desmarest, in their annoyance at Dubois' pretensions, gave him their support. In Fouché's bulletins the whole thing was reported as a mere episode, which had assumed larger proportions simply through Dubois' foolish simplicity, and through that alone could it disturb the general calm. Dubois soon submitted to the unanimous opinion, indignantly maintained by the other police authorities, which irritated and bewildered the Emperor. Thus on July 13 he wrote to Fouché : " Do not give me as much worry by yourself as the care of the whole empire would." No great treason trial followed, however ; nothing more happened than that Malet, with a few companions in misfortune, was put in prison for the time being.

Fouché, who had laid the storm, was esteemed even more than before by the former revolutionaries.

*　　*　　*　　*　　*

1809 proves a momentous year in Fouché's history. More than ever before he enjoys his Emperor's confidence, to be immediately after exposed to his unprecedented wrath. Amidst all this Fouché revives in a curious way the memories of his young manhood in Revolution times.

If Napoleon occasionally viewed Fouché's relations

with the Jacobins somewhat suspiciously, he yet, for the most part, looked upon his Minister's stormy past as a guarantee for his loyalty. Of this we have proof in what he once said to Fouché in a heated interview : " If a new revolution took place it would crush you to begin with, whatever part you might have taken in it." This was a remarkable utterance. Napoleon, severed from the Bourbons and their allies by the murder of Enghien and his followers, discussed the possibility of the former regicides deserting him for the enemy's camp. He perceived, however, that the Malet affair had given increased security to Fouché's secret position as leader for all in France who had any leaning towards the Left. Was it not better to bind this dangerous man to his own fortunes by giving him the highest public responsibility? Guided by some such politic thoughts as these, the Emperor allowed Fouché to keep his post when he himself hastened away in April to subdue Austria in her fresh attempt to take up arms against him, whilst the feud with Spain was still being fiercely carried on in the South. Indeed, when Cretet, the Minister of Internal Affairs, fell ill in June, Napoleon entrusted his office as well to Fouché.

An extraordinary situation at this time demanded extraordinary measures. Whilst ill-fortune seemed to attend the Emperor's sword, France was shaken by a monetary crisis. The general indignation at the ruthless levy of new troops was increased to a higher pitch by the agitation of the Catholic priests against imperial tyranny. Then Fouché interfered with wellnigh terrifying force, kept the Royalists and Catholics in check

176

without mercy, inspired financiers and manufacturers with fresh confidence, and stopped the fall of securities. The worst disturber of the peace, the Royalist Count de Noailles, was landed in prison. Thus Fouché suddenly became in all respects the driving-force in France, just as once upon a time, when Representative of the Convention, he had ruled Nevers and the surrounding district. When news came that the Emperor, on July 7, had conquered the Austrians' main force at Wagram, it seemed as though the dangers threatening his Empire, both from without and within, were averted for the present juncture, at any rate.

But at the same time Fouché received a reliable report of the formation of an English landing expedition, equipped with forty ships of the line, thirty frigates, eighty sloops of war and brigs, as well as four to five hundred transport-ships, with forty thousand men and one hundred and fifty cannon. It was evident that the attack was to be begun in the North against the tributary kingdom of Holland, set up by Napoleon for his brother Louis, along the lower course of the Rhine and the Scheldt. Fouché was very little worried, for he had, with all the care of an old schoolmaster, conscientiously repressed all opposition in these parts. Still, the risk was great enough, since some of the population in those districts had been, in the past, Austrian subjects, and were anxious to get back under their old Government, as well as being strongly Catholic into the bargain. Thus any English success would quickly enough kindle the fires of rebellion. The enemy did actually effect a landing on the island of Walcheren (July 29), quickly conquered the fortified

M

town of Middelburg, and set about besieging the chief defence on the island of Flushing, which fell into their hands on August 15. An attack was plainly imminent on the French northern base, Antwerp. The Emperor was still staying far away by the Danube; thus by a quick turn of fortune's wheel all was at stake.

On July 31 a Ministerial Council was summoned by the nominal head of the French Government, the former Consul, Cambacérès, now Arch-chancellor. But neither he nor Clarke, the Minister of War, had any other advice to offer than to make use of the few regular troops that they had within reach. Then all at once Decrès, the Naval Minister, threw out the suggestion that the citizen militia, the National Guards, should be levied in the old Jacobin way. But the Arch-chancellor and the Minister of War, who lacked initiative to do more than carry out mechanically the Emperor's orders, shrank from any such independent step. "I am not going to let myself be taken by the scruff of the neck, not I", Cambacérès is reported to have said. Fouché maintained a scornful silence during the Council, but after it was over, he, contrary to expectations, congratulated Decrès on his proposal, and without wasting any words told him that he himself now meant to act on his own responsibility.

On August 2 his colleagues heard, to their horror, that Fouché, on the strength of his double authority as Minister of Police and of Internal Affairs as well, had, without ado, called up the National Guards in fifteen departments. His experienced audacity went so far as to exclaim, in a circular letter to Prefects and Mayors: "Show Europe that even if Napoleon's

178

genius may lend splendour to France, yet his presence is not indispensable to repulse her enemies." The revolutionary fighting spirit really seemed to awake at the alarm call of the drums. The people flocked together as in Carnot's glorious days, and Fouché hastily assumed once more the dictator's fine airs of 1793. In Ghent twenty-five youths of wealthy families refused to be enrolled. The Minister of Police, with a grim face, requested a list of their names. But the higher officials in Paris, who were looking on helplessly at the trouble, could not control their fury, and Prefect Frouchot, at the head of the city Mayors, protested against the proceeding. Fouché replied with terrifying coolness that if he did not get their assistance in calling up the National Guards, "he would summon them himself with the sound of the drum". His opponents yielded. Fouché seems to have reached the height of audacity when he appointed the staff of officers for the Paris Militia, for, when complete, it consisted of nothing but opponents of Napoleon's system of absolute power, such as the banker Thornton at the head of the cavalry, and Stanislas de Girardin, an aristocrat of Liberal views, as Commander-in-Chief.

Perhaps Cambacérès and Clarke were even more horror-struck at the way in which the defence of Antwerp was arranged. For at Decrès' proposal Fouché appointed as Commander-in-Chief Bernadotte, the conspirator of 1802, who, moreover, had just been sent home in deepest disgrace by Napoleon, who disapproved of his self-assertive attitude at the battle of Wagram. And Bernadotte soon assumed the bearing of a dictator, ignoring the Minister of War and negotiating with Fouché only. In Antwerp he managed things according to his own fancy, making use of the local General Commissioner as his Minister for Internal Affairs. Meantime the French defensive measures were quickly consolidated, and the English troops were irresistibly forced to an ignominious defensive on Walcheren.

Fouché had thus, according to his custom—to quote Desmarest—combined with his greatest deeds certain of his own peculiar points of view, and these Napoleon could scarcely cancel without injury. To the great astonishment of many, the Emperor quickly took his part too, and without further ado confirmed, in a document dated August 8, not only the calling-up of the National Guard to a strength of thirty thousand men, but also Bernadotte's appointment as Commander-in-Chief at Antwerp. And more than this, Napoleon reproached Cambacérès and Clarke for letting themselves be caught napping, and plainly declared: "What is wanted is to stir up the nation to assert itself, first and foremost so that the English may lose their liking for such undertakings, and may be made to understand that the nation is always prepared to take up arms." This was to acknowledge that the Empire stood or fell in accordance with public opinion. The year before there had already been a hint of the same idea when Napoleon admonished the soldiers in Metz to conduct themselves well towards the civilians: "The French army is so excellent just because it is national." Although opposed to all Europe, the Emperor still hoped to be able to regain his strength on the lines of the French Revolution, whilst all the time his world-embracing plans estranged him more and more from the Frenchmen's attitude.

But the harmony between Napoleon and Fouché was broken soon enough. On August 15 the latter, in recognition of his services, had been made Duc d'Otranto (after the town on the south-east point of the Italian peninsula). In a coach, adorned with a coat of arms and with an escort of light cavalry, he now drove along, with the Duchess and his children at his side, to the Champ de Mars, where he held a parade of the National Guard, an unheard-of act of presumption in a Minister under imperial rule. With a persistence and arrogance which at all points remind us of the ex-Representative of the Convention, Fouché now endeavoured to fan the dying revolutionary flame throughout the whole of France. Under the pretext that English attacks might be expected on every coast, he had the National Guard called up in all departments, even down to Piedmont. Hulin, the military commandant in Paris, was furious that his guards were for ever coming upon strange patrols. The War Minister, Clarke, was greatly disturbed at seeing the command over the French fighting forces slipping out of his hands. In the Ministerial Council he openly stigmatized Fouché as " one of the Jacobins of 1793 ", a reproach to which the Police Minister retaliated by accusing Clarke of being in league with the English. It was an interchange of suspicion quite in accordance with the customs of Terrorist days. The report of these quarrels naturally woke manifold echoes in the Emperor's headquarters. As early as September 11 he took the command from Bernadotte, that man with

" growing aims " who lent a ready ear to the Paris
plotters. Fouché's actions gradually roused his fury,
particularly as the English still remained inactive. On
September 26 he thundered in a letter to the Minister
of Police : " What the devil do you mean by all this,
since there is no need and the thing cannot be done
without my orders ? " And he added nervously :
" Minds are growing uneasy, the least occurrence may
cause a crisis." Girardin was replaced by a reliable
man as Chief of the National Guard in Paris, and an
order given that their divisions in country places should
be disbanded to a great extent. On October 7 Fouché
lost his appointment as Minister of Internal Affairs.
As usual, he put a good face on a bad business. With
unparalleled nonchalance he was continually praising
his work to his confidante, Madame de Chastenay.
" The levy of the National Guard has strengthened
the Empire more than did the Coronation. Then he
was Emperor only by the power of the military, and
now the civil power has recognized him." Fouché, in
saying this, did not perhaps entirely forget that he
himself had once impressed on the public consciousness
that he himself and no other was in France the rightful
guardian of " the civil power ". But perhaps Fouché
ought also to have remembered that, for the present,
all power and authority in the land, and therefore his
position as well, rested, when all was said and done, in
the Emperor's hands. He had this time undoubtedly
challenged Napoleon by the cool and arbitrary manner
in which he had acted. It is true that the Emperor,
in a letter of October 21, spoke with recognition of
the great service rendered by the Minister of Police,

even if he had overstepped the legal boundaries. But when, a few days later, they met each other at Fontaine-bleau, Napoleon poured out his brooding indignation over his unfaithful servant, who owed everything to his master, but nevertheless, in his absence, played ducks and drakes with his money and goods.

Chapter XIX

The Bourbons, Talleyrand, Josephine

THOSE who try to follow the intricate workings of Fouché's activity will feel as though they are walking now through halls with secret passages in all the corners and hidden pitfalls at every step, now as if they have reached a deceptive room where the apparently clear views are but empty hallucinations and the figures they meet are only third- or fourth-hand reflections of the living forms they should represent. Such impressions as these are particularly strong when an attempt is made to explain Fouché's relations to Royalists and reactionaries during the Napoleonic rule.

When Fouché, in July 1804, again became Minister of Police, he noticed, to his horror, how imperfect was Napoleon's knowledge of the footing which the Bourbons' near and distant allies or their supporters had got in the country. His constant end and aim was to repair the damage, to keep the Emperor's suspicion turned on to the Right, and time after time to induce strong measures in that direction. But the strange point about it all was that the more success he achieved in this policy of his, the more favour he seemed to win in the eyes of those very people over whose heads he was calling down the lightning flashes of Napoleon's anger. It may appear incredible, but it is nevertheless a fact, that the Minister of Police at one and the same time was keeping alive the Revolution

CHATEAUBRIAND

From a print in the Bibliothèque Nationale

memories in France and creating a political base for himself in the Royalist camp ; indeed, he was preparing a secret anchorage for his influence even in Hartwell, Louis XVIII's English place of refuge. It was a balancing trick of consummate skill. In such a course of action Fouché was undoubtedly guilty of deep treachery to his master, the Emperor. And yet, more bewildering than all else, Fouché may be said to have worked as long as possible for the maintenance of Napoleon's empire, and not only this, but that in his arrogant and self-sufficient way he was more imperialistic in his policy than even the Emperor himself.

*   *   *   *   *

After a stay of some considerable time in Italy, Napoleon returned in July 1805 to Paris, distinctly disturbed by a number of private communications as to Fouché's intimacy with the Royalists in the faubourg St. Germain, where with sovereign ease he figured in the *salons* of the Marquise de Custine and of the wives of Vaudemont and de Chastenay and associated with fanatics like René de Chateaubriand. But Fouché, with his usual unconcern, now utilized his excellent sources of information and couched his bulletins in terms distinctly inimical to the Royalists, thus disarming Napoleon's wrath.

But when the Emperor, after the campaign in Moravia, saw his capital again in January 1806, he was no less dissatisfied with the Minister of Police, who was accounted responsible for the peace reports then in circulation. Fouché again took refuge behind his Royalist friends, and pointed them out as secret agitators.

A hundred of them were straightway arrested and banished to a distance of one hundred leagues from Paris. Several of the Royalists begged for pardon, and some of them were in fact cheered by the granting of their petition—apparently as a result of representations from Fouché, who in spite of everything proved himself a secret ally of Napoleon's victims. When, during the year 1807, the Chouans began plundering in Normandy, several of their friends amongst the Paris Royalists were thrown into prison, but Fouché, of course, carried out this measure in the Emperor's name, and maintained his own good relations with the Right. During all this, however, he used every effort to counteract the influence which the Royalists were beginning to gain amongst the country Communes, and also to prevent the repurchase of their confiscated property. Still more serious was the way in which Fouché, on several occasions, came into touch with the exiled Louis XVIII. It will be remembered how coldly his advances were repulsed in 1797. It is possible, although uncertain, that Fouché renewed his attempts both in 1803 and 1806, though probably only as a provocative measure.

An intrigue, the Perlet affair, concocted by the Minister of Police in 1807 to 1808, seems more suspicious. The idea at the beginning was that a poor creature, Fauche-Borel, a French political prisoner, had been set free under condition that he would spy on the French Royalists in other countries. But he afterwards had gone over into their service entirely. Fouché and his colleagues then relied instead upon another wretched individual, Perlet, who always enjoyed Fauche-Borel's full confidence. Perlet now communicated from Paris that a *comité royaliste* was being formed in France consisting of some of the most important of the military and civil officials in the Emperor's service, and that these were prepared at any time to overthrow Napoleon and summon back the Bourbons. It was now felt that Fauche-Borel must be enticed from London, where he lived, to make a secret visit to France, where his fate in that case would soon have been sealed. Fauche-Borel, however, took good care not to risk such an attempt to come into touch with the " Royalist Committee ", but he sent instead a young inexperienced kinsman of his, a Charles Vitel, who had to pay for his boldness with his life. Perlet, in spite of everything, maintained his friendly relations with Fauche-Borel, whom he convinced that Vitel had fallen by chance into the grip of the French police ; indeed, Perlet now, at the request of Fouché and his helpers, betook himself to London to the Bourbon headquarters, where the traitor met Louis XVIII himself, but otherwise was very unsuccessful in getting a hearing for his information, and had good cause to be thankful when he could return to Paris unharmed. The whole business was a clumsy intrigue of no great importance. What strikes us as amazing is the simple credulity and the profound ignorance of the position in France that was displayed by the Royalist leaders for so long a time. In this connection, the special point of interest is the firm confidence they showed in Fouché, in whom they imagined they had a sure and secret ally. Fouché's opponent, the Paris Prefect, Dubois, even hoped for a moment to get a dangerous weapon against him, when it got about that poor Vilet had brought with him, concealed in a stick, a letter to Fouché from Fauche-Borel. Fouché, all unconscious, took from Dubois' hands the letter, which turned out to be fairly non-committal. It must, however, have seemed very strange to Napoleon to see the high value that was placed in London on the influence of his Minister of Police. The idea of Fouché, the former regicide, being Louis XVIII's most trusted man in France was undoubtedly fantastic, but very possibly it did but confirm Napoleon's confidence in Fouché's extraordinary capability.

Fouché's attitude to the Catholic Church, resting as it did on the Concordat of 1802, was naturally of a very delicate nature. He, however, stuck to his opinion that the priests especially ought to work with the State authorities to maintain public order and morals. " This is more than a bond between your objects and mine ", was the ironical statement in the circular letter which Fouché sent to the bishops immediately after his rise to power in 1804. At the same time, like an echo from earlier times, came his declaration that a true religion was only such as succeeded in dispelling prejudices and superstition. When the priests touched on politics in their sermons they were severely reprimanded. Special religious societies Fouché could not endure. In his evident ill-will to the Jesuits he possessed an ally in Bonaparte, who ever since his youth had abhorred them in common with the various other monastic orders. Thus in the autumn of 1807 Fouché brought about the dissolution of the Society of the *Pères de la Foi*, a new manifestation in the Rhone Valley of the

Jesuit propaganda. Just as irreconcilable, although carried on in a less conspicuous way, was his contest with the clerical party at the Imperial Court under the leadership of Fontanes and Fiévée.

But when Napoleon's fight with the Papal power began, flaming up round the age-old question of the continuance or non-continuance of the Papal States in Italy, Fouché cautiously lowered his weapons. How could the Empire, already so infested by unrest and strife, endure this new shock? The Minister of Police tried, therefore, to the very last to modify the effect of Napoleon's fantastic persecution of Pius VII and his faithful followers. Consequently these Catholics heard with feelings of disappointment in the year 1810 that Fouché had been deprived of his office.

* * * * *

When Napoleon still retained Fouché as his Minister, in spite of his unexpected intimacy with the Royalists, his negligence in the Malet affair, and his arbitrary audacity in connection with the English attack at the mouth of the Scheldt, there must undoubtedly have been strong reasons to induce him to do so. It is scarcely sufficient explanation to point to Fouché's brilliant official routine or to the personal, wellnigh demoniacal power which he seems to have exercised over the Emperor, who was in many ways unsophisticated. The cause may rather have been the prominent part played by Fouché during those years in the prelude to Napoleon's divorce of his wife Josephine.

The reconciliation between General Bonaparte and his wife immediately before the *Brumaire coup* scarcely went to the very root of their trouble. Of an equable temper and tractable, Josephine, with her ready smiles and constant charm, certainly bore the ever-increasing burdens of her position and fulfilled the representative duties of Empress in an admirable manner. That no child was born of their marriage was, to begin with, of less importance, since Bonaparte at that time could scarcely know how long his power and splendour might last. His sisters meantime saw to it that the memory of Josephine's earlier lapse should not be entirely cast into the background, and the idea of divorce, which Napoleon had taken up so eagerly during his stay in Egypt, still remained in his mind as a vague possibility. Meantime it looked as if the question of Bonaparte's successor would be solved when, after the union in 1802 of Hortense, Josephine's daughter by her former marriage, with Louis, Napoleon's favourite brother, a son was born to them, and baptized with the names of Napoleon Charles, the last being after the First Consul's father. During all this Fouché still continued to fill the position of Josephine's confidant and friend, which he had assumed just before the *Brumaire coup*, and generous pecuniary help all the time came flowing in to Josephine from Fouché's funds.

The harmony was broken at last by two events. First, the Emperor Napoleon, who had doubted whether he would ever become a father, in December 1806, had a son born to him, the fruit of an irregular union. It was therefore possible that, if he repudiated Josephine, he might in another marriage be blessed with children. Next came the sad news that Napoleon Charles, to whom the Emperor was deeply attached, had died (in

May 1807), of croup. Since Napoleon's brothers could scarcely come into consideration as his successors, it now became necessary to make provision for the maintenance of the imperial power. The existing uncertainty of the matter directly invited the Bourbons and the hostile foreign Powers to hope that Napoleon would be killed in battle or got rid of in some way. Now Napoleon secretly had lists made of princesses suitable to replace Josephine as Empress. Fortunately, just at that time his campaign in the East culminated in the Franco-Russian peace at Tilsit. It appeared then a very possible suggestion that Napoleon's dynasty should be secured by a marriage between him and some Russian grand-duchess.

The initiative to Napoleon's divorce was at this point suddenly taken by Fouché, Josephine's sure refuge in so many storms. But just because he had been such a close friend, he proved a more formidable opponent to the Empress, well acquainted as he was with all her weaknesses, and in the eyes of the public the last who could be imagined as forsaking her, and who therefore could scarcely be supposed to do so without good reason.

The cause of this *volte-face*, so typical of Fouché, was fundamentally, no doubt, the fact that Josephine was only valuable as an ally in so far as she was indispensable to the Emperor and did not directly stand in the way of the maintenance of the Empire. But in both these respects the situation had now changed. Fouché, who felt his position threatened by many causes, then determined, without any scruples, to make capital out of the existing state of affairs, and by an unexpected, independent step to gain a fresh title-deed to Napoleon's gracious favour, whilst at the same time assuming the character before the whole world of champion for the diplomatic divorce. In November 1807 he visited the Empress in Fontainebleau, and, without any beating about the bush, exhorted her to express to the Senate her desire for a divorce. " The dynasty required it." But when the Empress asked Fouché if he was speaking at Napoleon's request, he was compelled to say no. Whereat Josephine naturally declared that only Napoleon himself had the right to demand such a thing from her.

In the explanation that followed between the imperial pair the Emperor yielded, overcome by the passion of the moment. He promised Josephine to give Fouché a good dressing-down—*lui laver la tête*—and the Minister of Police certainly did not get off scot-free. Napoleon was induced to write to Fouché, ordering him in future not to meddle with his family affairs. But the Minister was prepared for that, and accustomed to order his activities with a view to the distant future. Besides, for him there could scarcely be any turning back now that he had broken with Josephine and roused her anger. The Press suddenly began to discuss the question of the divorce, strongly advising a union with the Russian dynasty. There is no doubt that Fouché was at the back of this, for he would prefer France to be allied with the Russian Imperial House, destitute as it was of traditions, than with the Austrian, the very bulwark of *l'ancien régime* in Europe. In a significant way he endeavoured to draw Tolstoy, the recalcitrant Russian Ambassador in Paris, into his net, by exhorting him in the spring of 1808, if he wished to work for a rise in the Russian exchange, to spread the report of

Napoleon's approaching marriage with a Russian Princess.

The Emperor, who, in spite of continual disputes, again and again renewed affectionate relations with his wife under the irresistible influence of youth's ardent passion, was certainly not viewing Fouché with any favour, although he did not interfere with his policy. Indeed, when Napoleon, in the autumn of 1808, at the meeting of the Emperors in Erfurt, sought to enter into more friendly relations with Russia, it became evident that, in his heart of hearts, he shared the plans of his Minister of Police. But neither of them had any idea of the spirit of aristocratic superciliousness—especially due to the influence of the Russian Dowager Empress— which reigned in the innermost circles of the Petersburg Court, nor could they prevent Talleyrand, Napoleon's former Foreign Minister, who was secretly eager for an alliance with Austria, from gaining Czar Alexander's ear behind the scenes and persuading him not to become too deeply involved with Napoleon : " In Russia there is a civilized ruler at the head of a barbarous people, in France a barbarous ruler as leader of a civilized people." Should not then Alexander unite with Frenchmen to keep Napoleon's power within reasonable bounds? In short, the Erfurt meeting led to nothing for Napoleon.

*　　*　　*　　*　　*

The plans for a divorce were consigned to oblivion for the moment, but when the Emperor, in the autumn of 1808, led his eagles in person against the most dangerous districts of Spain, the question of the royal succession now for the first time became a serious and pressing one in the eyes of the Paris politicians. It was in this situation that Fouché and Talleyrand found each other, brought together by d'Hauterive, an old acquaintance from Oratorian days of Fouché's and at one time Talleyrand's right hand in the Foreign Office. " No one could believe his eyes ", it was said, when in December 1808 the two appeared in society arm-in-arm ; " crime supported by vice " was the verdict afterwards given. Fouché, that lower middle-class person, accustomed " to stick his dirty feet in any shoes ", and Charles Maurice de Talleyrand, blasé and superior, stamped from top to toe with an aristocratic lack of prejudice, who looked upon all intelligent means as equally good when it was a question of satisfying his consummate desire for pleasure, influence and wealth. If Talleyrand never ceased to be an *envoyé* after the style of *l'ancien régime*, who, even in Napoleon's service, with the unquestioned skill of a past-master in the art, represented the traditions of the old cynical cabinet policy, yet Fouché had steered his own course through the most tumultuous scenes of the Revolution, not indeed untouched by the spattering of its mud, but hardened and trained by the stern fight. Whilst Talleyrand's art consisted in utilizing the changing situations of imperial politics with no great effort or exertion, but with so much the surer instinct and elegant superiority, Fouché was a methodical worker, as indefatigable as skilful, a magnificent organizer, with a masterly understanding and sovereign control of the most difficult problems of internal government. But they were both equally wanting in any sense of the necessity of morality and of political propriety. This

194

alliance seemed the more astonishing since the innate mutual hostility between the two had, up till then, been looked upon as quite past reconciliation. Whilst Fouché after *Brumaire* remained a democrat with no reverence for tradition, Talleyrand had complacently greeted the return of social decorations to the public stage, even though he had driven Napoleon to his deed against Enghien that he might definitely bind him to the Revolutionaries. They both, however, regarded Napoleon's forceful political progress with similar mistrust and lack of enthusiasm. Desmarest reports verbally a conversation between the Emperor and his Minister of Police as follows : " What would you do, Fouché, if I met my death by a bullet or any other chance ? " " Sire, I would get as much power as I could to conquer events and not to be carried away by them." Napoleon (after a moment's consideration) : " Ah, well, that is quite in accord with the rules of the game." But why this public parade of intimacy between Fouché and Talleyrand, which could not fail to irritate the Emperor needlessly ? The real explanation is probably to be found in an attempt to show their own and foreign countries too that other Powers as well as Napoleon were playing their part in France.

The Emperor, who was secretly kept informed of everything, meantime hastened home. On January 17, 1809, he was in Valladolid, on January 22 in Paris. His loudly expressed wrath, however, was turned, in the first place, against the treacherous Talleyrand, who ever after became his implacable enemy, demanding, when his time came, like Shylock, his revenge even to the very last drop of blood. Fouché, too, had a warm quarter of an hour. But Napoleon still continued to believe in his loyalty, in spite of all, especially as Fouché was now working again for a divorce in the interests of the dynasty and making coarse and unworthy insinuations to Napoleon as to Josephine's frivolity, unreliability and foolishness.

*   *   *   *   *

The war with Austria broke out, and provided the Emperor with a double reason for carrying on his matrimonial schemes: first, the mortal danger to which he was exposed on the battle-field, and second, the anxiety for the future felt throughout France in connection with the landing of the English on the island of Walcheren. The personal tie between Napoleon and Josephine was already broken. In December 1809 the painful process of the public divorce was completed, and the Emperor stood ready to form a new union for the support of his tottering throne. Fouché had prepared public opinion on the divorce question. He still hoped the Emperor would fetch his bride from Russia, and gave expression to this view in the Imperial Council of January 23, where he was supported by Cambacérès and Murat. But no later than the beginning of February, Napoleon made a short and plain announcement that he had succeeded in winning the hand of the Archduchess Marie Louise, daughter of Francis I, Emperor of Austria. The miracle had happened : the insignificant Lieutenant of artillery, lifted to honour and glory by the same wave of revolution which had borne the daughter of the Hapsburgs, Queen Marie Antoinette, up to the scaffold, now once more united the destiny of France with the oldest monarchy of Europe.

Fouché's dreams had now certainly come to fulfilment. There was again a prospect of the continuance
of the Empire; but what about that Revolution legacy
which, up till now, the Minister of Police had guarded
as a dragon does his treasure in the fairy-tales? The
ranks of the Royalists grew closer and closer at
Napoleon's Court. We can easily believe in the statement that Fouché, in the spring of 1810, made to one
of his friends: "There is nothing left for me but to
pack my knapsack." But modesty was not Fouché's
strong point, and for the moment all seemed to be
working well. Fouché had good friends in the Austrian
diplomatic circles as well as here, there and everywhere
among Napoleon's former—and present—opponents.
It was noticed with amazement that the new Empress,
on one of her first evenings at Napoleon's Court, played
whist with Cambacérès and Fouché, both accomplices in
Louis XVI's death.

Bygones were bygones, so Fouché believed. His
foolhardy attitude is reflected in some words he is said
to have let fall to Thibaudeau, an old friend of his from
Convention days, immediately after the new Queen's
arrival in Paris: "She may perhaps prove as amiable
and attractive as her aunt. People have abused Marie
Antoinette and said many things against her, we most
of all. We were then standing in the stalls, ill-pleased
and difficult. At present we have really good places in
the best boxes. Let us applaud."

It would soon be apparent that Fouché had both
learnt and forgotten too little from his former "difficult" period to be any longer suitable for service under
the increasingly despotic rule of the Emperor Napoleon.

Chapter XX

Presumption and Fall

WHILST Napoleon in his French internal policy wavered between the feeling that he was heir to the Revolution and an unfortunate infatuation for the exaggerated refinements borrowed from *l'ancien régime*, his revolutionary methods became more and more pronounced in his attitude to other nations. With predestined directness he made an assault upon whatever was left from the past amongst the European States, did away with Austria's power in Northern Italy, disputed Russia's ruling influence in Central Europe, and looked upon England's supremacy upon the sea as a standing personal insult. In all this his course was influenced by motives of varying nature. Napoleon, who had won his spurs as a soldier of the Revolution, ever after contemplated Old Europe with a " new man's " distrustful glances. But the greater the success of his foreign policy, the higher his position, the more plainly he seemed to perceive that his work was part of a greater historical whole. For was not the empire which he had built in reality a manifestation of the world monarchy, that ideal for which his forefathers had once fought in the civil wars of the Florence Republic ? Thus Napoleon's ambition swelled into gigantic geographical proportions. As Fouché, in June 1808, candidly said to Metternich, the Austrian Ambassador in Paris : " Where can we find barriers against this scourge ? When he has begun a war with you, there still remains Russia, and after that China."

Since Fouché seriously considered the Empire as a rampart for the principles and for the upholders of the Revolution, Napoleon's war policy must, of course, have seemed to him nothing short of sheer madness, to put the matter plainly. By nature and unbridled habit Fouché interfered—as Talleyrand said—in everything that was his business and in everything that was not.

During his work as Ambassador in 1798 and 1799 he had, moreover, conceived an incurable liking for imperial diplomacy, which did but increase through his close contact, as Minister of Police, with international activities of a more or less suspicious character. And lastly, Fouché did not only speculate in political junctures, but on the Paris Bourse as well. The intimate relations which he formed in 1797 with rich members of the middle-class had been maintained to Napoleon's annoyance; the Emperor was especially irritated in the autumn of 1805 by Fouché's lucrative connection with that company of doubtful reputation, *Les Négociants Réunis*. But the cry of capitalists has always been for peace. It was the same chronic contradiction between the French imperial policy with its craving for war and French finance, making for peace, as recurred a hundred years later between Poincaré and Caillaux. Fouché, however, cleverly took advantage of his reliable sources of information to utilize Napoleon's successes for his own interests. When, in the summer of 1809, he flattered himself that he had restored the falling rate by an extensive purchase of stock, one of the contributory factors was that he had taken this step at the moment when he alone had received the news of the victory at Wagram.

Naturally Fouché also made use of his love of peace to increase his popularity. Thus he was known to have been at the back of the Senate's determination in the spring of 1807 to send a deputation to Poland to beg Napoleon to conclude a general peace. Public opinion in this was on the Police Minister's side; quite naturally, too, since he had himself made diligent use of his influence with the Press to induce it to adopt an attitude distinctly in favour of peace.

It seemed to Fouché that from every point of view a friendly agreement should be brought about with England, which, in the long run, was beyond the reach of Napoleon's weapons, but which, on the other hand, was continually inviting fresh European Powers to join in defensive measures against the encroachments of France, was impoverishing her industrial life and ruining her bankers by mercantile warfare, and was, moreover, never weary of fomenting disturbances within the French frontiers. It is true that now and again private negotiations had taken place between Napoleon and the English, but since the Emperor had devoted his efforts to the subjugation of Spain there was no apparent prospect of any agreement. The French, however, had suffered several reverses in Spain. If these continued, Napoleon might possibly be induced, at any rate on this front, to offer concessions to his opponents. The English Government would thus be able to call the attention of Parliament and of the general public to a success which might justify some conciliatory advances to France in other respects. Fouché may have reasoned in some such way as this. But did he not thus overlook the difficulty for England in any case to conclude actual peace as long as French swords were still flashing in the districts round the mouths of the Scheldt and the Rhine? At all events he determined to make secret attempts to establish relations with the English statesmen, so that when a suitable opportunity arose it might be easier to effect a *rapprochement* between them and Napoleon.

It was a hazardous game indeed, a manifestation of that almost morbid desire to interfere in the affairs of others which had always distinguished Fouché. Should he, who had weathered the storm in the Malet affair, who had acted as master in France during Napoleon's absence in 1809 without incurring any punishment, and who now was received at the Court of the former Archduchess of Austria—should he not be able to guide his country's destinies beyond her frontiers? The discretion which in the period from 1797 to 1807 marked Fouché's conduct seems to have utterly disappeared. His political imagination treats questions of great weight as if they were but insignificant money investments; his statecraft is thus driven on to uncontrolled foolhardiness. Fouché's way grows dark and the autumn is near!

Fouché had already used his secret police connections in England for private aims of his own when, in November 1809, he began to treat with a Captain Fagan, a former *émigré*, whose elderly father was still living in London. The Minister of Police represented to him the possibility of a journey to England. He was to take this opportunity to visit, on Fouché's behalf, the Under Foreign Secretary, Wellesley, and put before him the desirability of bringing about a *rapprochement* between

France and England. Fagan, who considered the matter worthy of the most earnest consideration, and who believed Napoleon to be cognizant of what was proposed, willingly fell in with Fouché's proposal. In the end of January 1810 he succeeded, too, in carrying it out, but found Wellesley inclined to be very cautious, for the Emperor seemed just then as though he intended to incorporate Holland in France. Moreover, any agreement would be impossible if Spain did not take part in it as an independent State. Fagan's negotiation thus came to nothing. He himself was too sickly to be able to undertake any more of Fouché's errands ; the latter, however, informed him that "Napoleon was satisfied" with the way he had carried out his commission.

Quite unintentionally Napoleon himself now came to the help of his Minister's intrigues. Strengthened by the assistance of his father-in-law, the Austrian Emperor, he was now quite determined not only to subdue Spain but to incorporate with his own country his dependent kingdom of Holland, which was to be entirely debarred from all mercantile relations with England. But England was to bear the blame of this last measure. Consequently Napoleon allowed the Dutch Government to enter into secret negotiations with the English, to inform them of the Emperor's incorporation schemes, and to hint that these might possibly be laid aside if only England would grant greater freedom to French trade. The proposal was hopeless, since, from the English standpoint, it was a question of the greatest indifference as to how far Napoleon directly or—as hitherto—indirectly governed Holland. It was, however, very significant that Fouché had the management of the secret negotiations between

Amsterdam and London. It so happened that he applied for information to Ouvrard, a speculative banker of the Directory period, who had offended Napoleon, been shut up for a time in Vincennes, and now was anxious to get back into the Emperor's good graces and also to do some profiteering for himself on the conclusion of peace. Ouvrard pointed out as a suitable intermediary the Dutchman Labouchère, head of the Hope banking-house in Amsterdam and son-in-law to Baring, one of the directors of the English East India Company. These were two of the principal figures in the international financial world of those days to whom Fouché thus had recourse—the same broad-minded business men who, later on, were to get France invaluable credit during the difficult years of 1815 to 1818. Now Labouchère did, in fact, undertake to arrange the negotiation—with the negative result already mentioned. In the end of February 1810, as a punitive measure, great parts of Holland were incorporated in the Empire of France.

Fouché thereupon took over Napoleon's rôle in his relations to Labouchère, who, however, seems to have had no idea that Fouché was now acting on his own authority. On the other hand, Ouvrard, who was still acting as intermediary, may have known of the deception. But this man was nothing but an adventurer, who did not mind putting a good face on a bad business if there was the slightest chance of making the least profit out of it. Fouché, in short, persuaded Labouchère that Napoleon, in consequence of his marriage, was inclined to make important concessions to his opponents. This time it was not to be the Dutchman himself but his father-in-law, Baring, who was to come into touch with

Wellesley. The intrigue has one touch of originality about it, namely, the idea that the French should help the English to subdue the rebellious North Americans and in return receive Spain's former transatlantic colonies. When Baring, at the beginning of April, had an interview with Wellesley, his proposals met with a sympathetic reception, so much so that Baring, on the 17th of the same month, was in a position to tell Labouchère that the English Government thought the proposition useful as a basis for negotiation. Fouché, moreover, had got into England's good books by releasing on his own responsibility one of their agents, Baron Kolli, whom he had arrested. But then, all at once, suspicion seems to have been aroused; on May 8 Wellesley said to Baring that nothing could be effected unless the French Government sent over a plenipotentiary, and also that it was feared that the negotiations would be useless for the present.

In the beginning of April, Fouché wrote to Labouchère that the proposal to the English Government " has been read with great attention " and considered " tactful and suitable ". Labouchère consequently believed that his course of action had met with the Emperor's approval. But Ouvrard for his part made an additional effort to open Napoleon's eyes to what was going on by sending a communication to him in which he advised that the French should try to get possession of North America, so that they could put up a stronger opposition to England from there—that is, the exact opposite to the scheme which had been propounded to the English. The Emperor naturally took scant notice of Ouvrard's fantastic scheme, but he may have harboured a suspicion

204

that there was some intrigue about it. Perhaps Fouché, in his customary free and easy manner, now intended to tell Napoleon the whole history as one of his usual tricks to tempt an enemy on to thin ice. The Emperor, to be sure, had once before joined in the laugh when Fouché had told how smartly he had brought about discord between Louis XVIII and the English Ministers. But the unlucky "circumstances" which had so often given the Police Minister unexpected support in slippery places suddenly failed him. When the Emperor in May was on his magnificent wedding-tour in Belgium and met his brother, King Louis, the latter happened to mention that he had met Ouvrard, who was travelling from Amsterdam to Paris to get fresh instructions from Fouché for the negotiations with England. Napoleon was startled; he may possibly have remembered Ouvrard's latest project; at any rate he scented the whole matter and gave vent to a terrible outburst of rage against the intriguers. That over, he came to his senses as usual and set himself resolutely to prepare for the next scene by collecting inculpating evidence against the culprits. He forbade all intercourse between Ouvrard and Labouchère, and got Louis to question the latter, who in full confidence revealed practically everything.

Ouvrard continued to rely on Fouché's putting everything right, and advised the Minister of Police always to use Labouchère as intermediary in the relations with England. Fouché, moreover, received full information as to the state of affairs from Malouet, an ex-Oratorian, now Prefect in Antwerp. But the last hour had struck of Fouché's second term of office. What did Napoleon care if the English Government shrank still more from treating with him, when he revealed their simplicity in falling into Fouché's trap? On his return to Paris he summoned, on June 2, 1810, all his Ministers and higher dignitaries to a Council meeting. The Emperor turned to Fouché: "You now rule over war and peace?" The Minister of Police kept cool, but condescended at least to grant that the banker Ouvrard was a common intriguer—exactly as once, seventeen years before, he had in the Jacobin Club denied Chaumette, his secret comrade of Nevers. It was no use. Whilst Fouché was detained by the meeting Napoleon had Ouvrard arrested in spite of his protests and succeeded in confiscating all his papers. The Emperor's wrath rose automatically: "Duc d'Otrante, you ought to give up your head on the scaffold," he broke out in the course of the meeting. Then turning hastily to his Minister of Justice, he inquired: "What do the laws say of a Minister who treats with the enemy without his sovereign's knowledge?" And the answer was: "Your Majesty has already said. The law is explicit in that case."

Fouché's downfall was now imminent. Certainly it may be said that he had come to grief by his own fault— his passionate love of power and his undisciplined weakness for interference. But at the same time it must be acknowledged that his movement for peace was the outcome of an indispensable political necessity, the desire for moderation in the revolutionary foreign policy which once found expression in Danton's programme touching the "natural boundaries". Uncertainty and misgivings for the future were meantime as great amongst Fouché's friends as amongst his enemies. The general feeling was excellently voiced by no one less than Talleyrand, who is reported to have said in an undertone to his neighbour : " Without doubt Fouché has done very wrong. I for my part would give him a successor, but only one, i.e. Fouché himself." So inextricably united had the Minister of Police and his office become in public opinion generally. Yet half a decade was to elapse before the two came together again—dark, gloomy years in the history of France and of Fouché alike. Napoleon had by degrees taken all influence from his brother Lucien, Talleyrand and Fouché—all three his former independent co-operators in 1799. Defiant in his autocracy and military success, he no longer tried, as in 1809, to draw strength from revolutionary sources. Thus Fouché's incalculable and baffling power could not find any further place in Napoleon's stiff political system, and he was replaced as Minister of Police by Savary, one of his " Mamelukes ", a go-ahead fellow with an exclusively military training. But the forces of the past, awakened to life by Enghien's fate, gathered together by degrees in self-defence against the Corsican's stormy advance.

Chapter XXI

The Collapse of the Empire
and the Rule of the Bourbons

NAPOLEON's wrath had taken Fouché by surprise, otherwise he would certainly have been better prepared to leave his office. Now he and his confidant, Gaillard, were fully occupied for several days in burning masses of compromising papers and letters, whilst Savary, the new Minister of Police, awaited Fouché's departure with respectful patience. Fouché had been nominated Governor-General of Rome, and was preparing to act with pomp and state the part of Dictator in Middle Italy after his usual fashion. But meantime the report of the paper-burning in the police ministerial offices reached Napoleon's ears, who, moreover, was gradually grasping the full extent of Fouché's foreign intrigues. So Fouché's honourable retirement was changed into deep disgrace, and he was banished on July 1 to his *sénatorerie* of Aix, and directed to hand over immediately all the written communications and letters that he had received from Napoleon. Fouché first retired to his estate at Ferrières, near Paris, and persistently maintained that all such documents had been burnt. In reference to this matter, Fouché said to Réal in his usual high-flown manner : " I have never looked for any other safeguard than in the Emperor's heart and in my own conscience." Since the Emperor at least had no confidence in the latter, but, on the contrary, showed signs of violent

FOUCHÉ IN HIS OLD AGE

Lithograph from "Le Secret de Fouché," by E. Forgues

displeasure, Fouché at last lost his self-control and fled, head over heels, to Italy, going indeed so far as to embark on August 7 in Leghorn, with the idea, so it was said, of emigrating to America. He turned back, however, at once, perhaps owing to terrible sea-sickness, to which Fouché, a sea captain's son from Brittany, fell a victim, but possibly, too, of set purpose, for he had written to the Emperor immediately before, begging for pardon. His attempt at flight, then, was no more than a gesture to show Napoleon how troublesome it might be to have a man like Fouché in the enemy's camp. At the same time his wife delivered into the Emperor's hands some of the letters in dispute.

The sequel was that Fouché, in September, had to betake himself to Aix, an object of Napoleon's contemptuous pity. It was political shipwreck, but this time, in contrast to 1795, without pecuniary straits as well, for Fouché's means in landed property alone amounted to about fifteen million francs, apart from the sum total of £120,000 of interest which in the course of years had been paid to him from Government funds. Fouché, who at other times despised luxury and superfluity, now lived like a king in his province, made much of even by the nobility living on the neighbouring estates, amongst whom the family of the ex-Prince Castellane took an important position. Also a young lawyer, Manuel, attracted Fouché's notice by his eloquence, talent and enthusiasm for the ideals of the Revolution and remained his friend in the future. In October 1811 Fouché received permission to visit his castle of Ferrières. He had always followed with interest all political happenings, and now he was allowed

from time to time to put forward his views personally
to the Emperor and to warn him against extensive war
operations, and particularly against the Russian campaign
in 1812. But Fouché devoted himself to his family
before all else. His wife's health had long been failing,
and Bonne-Jeanne died on October 9, 1812, sincerely
and bitterly mourned by her husband. He bore testimony to a friend of how she had shared his life, his
work, his reading, his walks, his rest, his sleep—
" everything we shared ". For this strange man, who
always combined the career of an unconscientious and
coldly calculating politician with an intimate and affectionate family life, his wife's death must have been a
terrible blow. The icy restless spirit of his public life
now pervaded his whole existence.

* * * * *

With the end of the year 1813 Napoleon's power
began to show signs of waning. He returned from his
Russian adventure with only the remnants of his mighty
army, and again the European Powers collected to do
battle with the tyranny of France. Even her ally
Austria seemed prepared to go over to the enemy.
Every man still left who was capable of bearing arms
was summoned to rally round the French banners.
Would it not have been possible for Napoleon at the
last moment to make favourable terms with his enemies,
who in many things were still mutually at variance ?
If we may believe Madelin's last description of the
general state of affairs in the Empire, Napoleon's reputation must have been so great in France, his position so
strong, his benefits to the French nation so numerous,
that he could certainly have reconciled his people to

very considerable sacrifices in their foreign policy. When Napoleon, in spite of this, did not try to treat with his opponents, but preferred to defend his enormous conquests to the very last, he acted as an implacable fighter, a soldier of fortune, not as a European statesman. But the French enthusiasm of an earlier date had grown cold under the breath of reaction. Napoleon, who was preparing for a stern and decisive struggle in mid-Europe, was afraid that a revolution might break out—once his back was turned—in France, where the Empress Marie Louise was to assume the reins of government during his absence. In May 1813 he therefore summoned Fouché to Dresden, under the pretext of putting him in charge of his Prussian possessions.

The meeting between Napoleon and Fouché throws a strange light on the position of the French in the Europe of that day. How one-sided was the way in which they regarded their contests, victories and defeats as affairs in which France alone was concerned! How ruthlessly they stirred up foreign Powers to serve their private passions! In 1805, when Russia and Austria united their forces against Napoleon, general attention was aroused by the French *émigré*, Comte d'Antraigues, when he issued a pamphlet comparing the Emperor with the Roman conquerors who utilized the Syrians' (Prussians') and the Macedonians' (Austrians') mutual strife to establish their empire. Still more eloquent is another incident. Bernadotte, the French general who conspired against Napoleon in 1802, and during his absence in 1809 placed himself at the head of the national defence movement, had, in the following year, accepted the succession to the Swedish throne, so that he might in that position continue the campaign against his old rival. At all events, this was the interpretation put upon his action by several of his compatriots. The memoirs of Desmarest, Head of the Secret Police, offer a striking illustration of this. In the autumn of 1812, when the Emperor was penetrating the vast solitude of the Russian steppes and his subjects at home were anxiously awaiting the outcome of his struggle with Czar Alexander and his ally Bernadotte, now Crown Prince of Sweden, General Malet, the conspirator of 1808, once again endeavoured to carry out a *coup d'état* in Paris under the pretext that Napoleon had been killed. Malet triumphed for two short hours. When Desmarest was taken with others to the prison of La Force he pictured to himself—so he relates— "Bernadotte in the Emperor's Russian camp, arriving after the fatal shot, to offer himself as intermediary to our irresolute generals, establishing with them a new Government under the protection of Alexander, after he had sent off to Paris the instructions that had been agreed upon and messages with the same end in view." Desmarest soon saw his mistake, and Malet paid with his life for his *idée fixe*.

When, the year after, the French's statesmen and soldiers really saw the Crown Prince amongst their opponents, they sometimes looked upon the whole war as a continuation of the internal risings in their own country. Even Napoleon said to Fouché in Dresden— if the Minister's memoirs are to be believed—" I know all ambition and passion is roused against me. Your Bernadotte, for example, can do us much harm by giving our enemies the key to our policy and tactics." Fouché,

Bernadotte's former friend—and perhaps at that moment too—feeling uncomfortable, doubtless not without reason, replied : " Bernadotte will certainly shine in Germany, but France he will never attack." Napoleon, however, declined to recognize this distinction between Bernadotte's military power and his love for his mother-country: " *Bah! la France! la France! c'est moi!* " And once again these old disputants argued over their different political principles, Napoleon maintaining that the war must be fought to a finish, since " our political supremacy is at stake ", whilst Fouché voiced the necessity of buying Austria's favour by generous evacuation of land, by an immediate retirement within French frontiers, and an endeavour to stamp out in the classic revolutionary ground the sparks of the enthusiasm for defence—as in the year 1809,

In actual reality, however, Napoleon's and Fouché's conversation was but empty words, for the Emperor's one aim in it all was to get the dangerous man under his own supervision. He let him for appearance' sake write to Bernadotte, and when no result followed, he sent him in August to treat with Metternich in Prague, an errand that also proved abortive. Fouché, who no longer believed in Napoleon's lucky star, made use of the opportunity to recommend that the Emperor's son by Marie Louise should take his father's place on the French throne under the guardianship of his mother. Then Fouché, by Napoleon's order, travelled far from the centre of activities to take up the post of Governor-General of the French Illyrian Provinces. When, in the autumn of 1813, Napoleon's banners wavered and fell on the battle-fields of Germany, French rule was overthrown in Fouché's provinces as well. He, however, maintained his supercilious coolness amidst all difficulties, and cleverly led the retreat of his fellow-countrymen into Italy. There he at once found new and trying tasks awaiting him.

* * * * *

In the great rearguard battle at Leipzig Napoleon's mighty reputation received its death-blow, and the field of competition was now open for the three antagonistic forces that, before the Empire, had contended with each other for the mastery in France, viz. the ill-used Bourbon dynasty, the veterans of the Revolution, and the soldiers who had been trained in the French republican army from 1790 to the end of the century. Under Napoleon's rule, too, these parties had occasionally made their presence apparent. Thus the ex-regicide Fouché, in 1802, and also in 1809, had, quite independently of Napoleon, entered into relations with Bernadotte and Murat. In the imperial army, too, the ex-Revolution generals had always taken a high and insolent tone as well as exercising an entirely arbitrary rule within their command. When Napoleon's iron hand dropped the reins, it was to be expected that these soldiers, accustomed to obey only under certain provisos, would all take their own way. Even before this, Murat, brother-in-law to the Emperor, and appointed by him vice-King in Naples, had been suspected of attempts in this direction. Now, when all was in jeopardy, Napoleon sent Fouché to Murat with directions to bring up all available troops and to join the main French army in Northern Italy under command of Eugène de Beauharnais.

It is uncertain how Fouché carried out his errand. Now, however, that his worst misgivings of Napoleon's powerlessness had been realized, it is scarcely credible that Fouché would very emphatically dissuade Murat from failing his brother-in-law in his need. When Murat, in January 1814, openly deserted Napoleon to join his opponents, Fouché admonished him, above all, to form a good and efficient army, or else he would in any case be despised. Thus it is plain that—as the events had shaped themselves—Fouché hoped Murat would eventually play an important part in the decision of the question of the future government of France. Perhaps he remembered his plans in 1809 of forming, in the event of Napoleon's fall, a new Government with the help of just such a celebrated soldier as Murat. Murat, however, proved useless. Events in France took a headlong course, and Napoleon was deposed. His son was out of the running, too, and the Bourbons were at last masters of the land. In the new Government then formed, Talleyrand, Fouché's old ally of 1809, was the leading spirit. So matters stood when Fouché, on April 6, again made his appearance in Paris.

*　　　*　　　*　　　*　　　*

Fouché did not look upon the situation as very tragic. His period of police ministry appeared in the light of almost romantic gentleness and humanity compared with Savary's disagreeable military methods. His well-preserved underground apparatus for treating with the Royalists was brought into use again and acted excellently. He was evidently an influential and dangerous fellow, who ought not to be offended.

Just as the Senate at one time had decided on Napoleon's promotion to imperial power, so now they demolished his rule. Fouché, in consequence, hastened to take his seat as Senator. Talleyrand and he soon joined hands in a common effort to turn the

misfortune into the best that was possible for France—
and for themselves ! Was the difference between 1814
and *Brumaire* so unfathomable ? Fouché, at all events,
had to begin from the beginning again. Just as fifteen
years before he had tried to impress his radical political
teaching on the vainglorious Corsican, now he had to
undertake the education of the Bourbons in the necessary
respect for the work of the Revolution. One merit at
least the fresh rulers possessed : they understood that
it was no easy task to rule the new France, whilst
Napoleon, to end with, had paid but little heed to the
ideals left to the heirs of the Revolution.

Fouché never wearied of reminding the Royalists, and
through them Louis XVIII, that the new kingdom was
not the same as the former monarchy, that Louis XVIII,
unlike his forefathers, was unknown to the greater part
of his people, and that he must keep a check upon those
passions which had germinated in him and his followers
during their exile, if all was to go well. Did not the
glorious Revolution of 1688 follow the hardly-won
Restoration in England ? These were exactly the same
views which Talleyrand, after the July Revolution of
1830, was to emphasize with such masterly diplomacy
during his renowned embassy to London. With a
skilful hand Fouché shaped his old defence of the effect
and ideas of the Revolution into accord with the new
time. Honest compensation must be made to the
returning *émigrés* for their lost property, or else the
present occupiers would be tortured by constant anxiety.
When Fouché thus endeavoured to work for general
reconciliation, he often used to philosophize over the
changed times. For instance, on one occasion he
wrote to Louis XVIII's brother, the Comte d'Artois :

" The thing of greatest moment to France and to Europe, for which we ought to make every sacrifice, is quietness for her people and rulers after so much unrest and distress." This was Fouché's old message of peace, arrayed in a new garb, a ghost of the enthusiasm for universal material prosperity, but a proof, too, that Fouché had grasped the master-passion of the new time. Indeed, he zealously maintained that the age of industry and trade had come. His earlier enthusiasm for liberty, equality and fraternity had now been changed into enthusiasm for the progress of material civilization. In this we see a striking reflection of the course of his own personal development from 1793 to 1814.

But Fouché preached to deaf ears, a result that did not exactly please him, and this time he did not by any means become, as he hoped, the Minister of Police in France. Louis XVIII, that sceptical, practical politician, no doubt, as far as he personally was concerned, would have capitulated from motives of expediency, but he was prevented by consideration for the Duchesse d'Angoulême, Louis XVI's daughter, " the only man in the family ", as Napoleon said. Consequently, Fouché, for the present, had to continue to occupy himself with his own domestic affairs. Meantime reaction grew and manifold interference with those of like views with himself. So Fouché got so far as to " wish for any revolution, whatever it might be ", to quote Barras' words. If the Bourbons had learnt nothing of the new time's message, neither had Fouché forgotten any of his former art in tripping up, all unnoticed, those rulers who wielded their power unskilfully. Barras, mentioned just above, may have been able to whisper a hint of this to Louis XVIII.

Chapter XXII

The " Hundred Days " and the Second Restoration

IN September 1814 Fouché, in a letter to a French
diplomat, made the bold assertion that the Revolution
had maintained a peaceful attitude to foreign Powers,
and that it was Napoleon who had beguiled the French
into warlike adventures. As early as April he had tried
to induce the Bourbons to use their influence against
the proposal to let the Emperor find a place of refuge
on the island of Elba, "where he will be for Italy,
France, the whole of Europe, what Vesuvius is for
Naples " ; he ought rather to be banished to North
America, to learn there the meaning of national freedom.
Fouché kept his view to the last that Napoleon, as a
power, was quite worn out, and would henceforth only
rouse up political unrest and disturbance. Talleyrand
took up the same standpoint when representing France
at Vienna, where the Powers had to settle the future of
Europe. How comes it then that Fouché makes his
appearance as one of Napoleon's Ministers when the
latter, in March 1815, drives away the Bourbons from
France ? Two mishaps that befell Fouché fully explain
how this happened. Even if Fouché did not wish for
Napoleon's return, on the other hand he wanted to
depose the Bourbons at any price. Whilst he was
simply notifying to the police authorities the conspirators' plans to fetch the former Emperor from Elba,
he was plotting on the opposite side with the military

218

commander in Lille, General Drouet d'Erlon, who was to march upon Paris and put an end to the rule of Louis XVIII. Fouché probably intended as the next step to raise Napoleon's son by Marie Louise to the throne, relying for this on Metternich's support. When the message came that Napoleon had landed in the South of France, Fouché fired his mine too in order to get rid of both the Bourbons and Napoleon at one and the same time, but with little result. Drouet d'Erlon could not effect his march on Paris.

In addition to this disappointment there came a narrow escape from being put under lock and key for an indefinite period. When the Bourbons' rule was coming to grief they hastened, at last, to offer Fouché the post of Minister of Police. On hearing his answer that it was "too late", they feared treachery on his part and proceeded to arrest him on the morning of March 16. Fouché, however, disconcerted the police by declaring that it was all due to a misunderstanding, got a moment's breathing-space, took flight through a trap-door in his Ministry building, and managed to get into a neighbouring back-yard. "As by a miracle in an Arabian fairy-tale, I saw myself suddenly in the midst of the Bonapartist innermost circle," Fouché narrates in his memoirs. For the house and garden happened to belong to Hortense, Napoleon's stepdaughter by his first marriage.

In an instant black had become white, and Fouché, the shady character, a martyr for Napoleon's cause! The ex-Emperor, who on his triumphal course through France had planned that Savary should again be his Minister of Police, found it advisable to fall back on his old opponent for this appointment. Fouché, as usual, would have preferred to become Minister of Foreign Affairs. It is, however, almost, if not quite, the most suspicious point in Fouché's varied existence that, in spite of his inward conviction that the new Government was inevitably doomed, he yet endeavoured to obtain a leading post in it. He was also guilty of twofold treachery to his master, first by insuring himself against Napoleon's despotism by fostering a lively opposition to him amongst his countrymen, and second, in securing his own future safety by forming close connections, behind Napoleon's back, with his enemies, the Bourbons and Austria. We cannot, therefore, in any way blame French patriots for considering that Fouché's policy meant an unconscientious weakening of his country's strength just when she was going to meet terrible dangers under the leadership of the man who, in spite of all, had covered the French flag with undying glory.

A racy episode of Fouché's artful game behind the scenes deserves mention here. Metternich, with whom Fouché was plainly in treaty in May, sent a message to the Police Minister that an Austrian agent, Baron Ottenfels, had gone to Basle to meet Fouché's emissaries. Napoleon, however, intercepted this greeting and let one of his men, Fleury de Chaboulon, figure in Basle as Fouché's messenger. Fleury ascertained that the Powers would prefer any Government whatsoever in France rather than Napoleon's rule, and that Fouché was secretly treating with Metternich, although he could discover no other fresh criminal facts in the Police Minister's dealings. Meantime Fouché appears to have got wind of the contra-espionage, and condescended personally to tell

Napoleon that he had received a letter from Metternich. Probably it was on this occasion that Napoleon exclaimed to his disloyal servant : " Fouché, you are a traitor. I ought to have you hanged." To which Fouché replied with grim humour : " I am not of Your Majesty's opinion."

Fouché seems, moreover, to have acted with sublime impartiality an equally deceitful part towards both Napoleon and the Bourbons, betraying the former's actions to his enemies and revealing the Bourbon confidences to the French Council of War.

Yet, in spite of everything, we must acknowledge that Fouché did his best to make the difficult transition period of the " hundred days " as painless as possible for the French people, and that he used all his power to restrict political persecutions. Of course there were threatening signs of a Chouan rising on a grand scale, but the Minister of the Police succeeded in reducing its importance and violence by skilful negotiations with its leaders. The fate of France was to be decided on the battle-fields of Belgium. These efforts of Fouché, too, certainly had another side, in his personal concern that as little bloodshed as possible should stand between him and the Bourbons.

Fouché now made his début in a new rôle, which he played with masterly skill—that of parliamentary leader of the Opposition. Openly or secretly he had so influenced the election for the Chamber of Representatives, which was now summoned, that it had a majority of a distinctly Liberal character. Had not Fouché, in January 1814, written to Murat, that the outcry for a Constitution meant nothing more than " a vague wish not to obey " ! Amongst the Representatives there appeared, side by side with celebrated Revolutionaries, Manuel, the Police Minister's friend since his days of exile in Aix, ready with keen-edged, eloquent criticism of Napoleon's rule. Thus Fouché prepared if necessary to check the Emperor as in bygone times he had circumscribed Robespierre's influence in the Convention before *Thermidor*.

Napoleon's keen eye saw through Fouché's attitude, but he preferred calmly to await the decision of arms before he attacked the Police Minister's strongly fortified positions. Then the tragic day of Waterloo dawned and sealed the Emperor's fate. Fouché might flatter himself on having been a true prophet, but his satisfaction was terribly clouded by learning at once that there was no prospect of succession to the throne either for Napoleon's son or for the Duke Louis Philippe of Orleans, the Liberal member of the former Royal House. The Council of the Powers had irrevocably resolved that Louis XVIII should once more assume his full authority. Thus poor, shattered France was threatened with much misery at the hands of the foreign soldiers who were to reinstate the Bourbons, and also of their devoted followers, whose hatred of the upholders, both of the Revolution and the Empire, had blossomed and grown to great dimensions during their time of humiliation and exile. Yet at this juncture—as De La Garce has emphatically pointed out—the return of the moderate and shrewd Louis XVIII was the only conceivable method to save France from being torn asunder by foreign Powers or completely disorganized by internal anarchy, the only guarantee that, considering everything, could be given for the maintenance of the kingdom as such. The situation was one of such peculiarity that although the Bourbons were brought back to Paris by the force of foreign Powers, they yet formed the only practical possibility of defence against the misuse of this force.

Fouché fearlessly applied himself to the thankless task of softening down the sharp contrast between what had been and what was to come. It must be confessed that he possessed unique qualifications for this office in his ambiguous relations with both camps. In any case his policy from June 19, when the news of Wagram reached him, until July 8, when Louis XVIII returned to Paris, was the masterly feat of a skilled artist, a wonderful exhibition of rope-dancing over dizzy heights and depths, unequalled even in his own amazing history. These events can only receive a passing mention here.

When Napoleon returned from the battle-field, prepared to begin a civil war, Fouché incited the Representatives still more fiercely against him to tie his hands and prevent all useless bloodshed. With significant audacity he, by means of notes actually written in the midst of the interminable Government Council meetings, directed the manœuvres of the parliamentary Opposition. Hence it was no mere chance when his confidant and friend, Manuel, denounced Napoleon from the Speaker's platform as the only cause of the war, and threw out the suggestion of his compulsory abdication. His Ministers were all seized by the general panic, and the Emperor, weary of contest, retired for ever. In the Chamber of Representatives Fouché was still regarded

as the persistent opponent of the Bourbons, so that
when a Government Commission of five members was
appointed he was made chairman. Whilst the Parlia-
mentarians were now most anxious for Napoleon II to
succeed to the throne, Fouché tried to get a general
idea afloat that the Bourbons would nevertheless have
to return. He thus induced Davout, the War Minister,
to declare publicly that Louis XVIII must be recognized
if Frenchmen wished to avoid the disgrace of his being
raised to the throne of France by means of foreign
bayonets. In vain! The Chamber of Representatives
began to suspect Fouché's double-dealing, and violent
threats were hurled at him by Bonapartists and Republicans alike. In the Government Commission Fouché
was bitterly attacked by Carnot, his colleague, the
well-known organizer of peace of 1793, who was just
as intolerant now as then of veiled hints and subterfuges.
The foreign generals, above all the Prussian Blücher,
who meantime had pitched his camp near Paris, were
growing impatient at the delay. Then Davout's old
fighting spirit awoke once more. How desperate the
situation would be if the foreign Powers now completed
their victory and the Bourbons returned as symbol and
proof of the irresistible triumph of the forces of reaction!
Fouché redoubled his efforts, explained to his environment the dangers of the position, moderated in private
the desire of the foreigners for war, and at last, on
July 3, brought about a capitulation which allowed
Louis XVIII to take possession again of his former
kingdom. It could not be helped that foreign troops
marched into Paris as the royal body-guard. At
the same time the Government Commission came to

an end, and the Chamber of Popular Representation was dissolved.

*   *   *   *   *

Even if Fouché's action in the Government Commission had been suspicious in many respects, yet it seems as if we must believe, just for this once, his explanation concerning his relations with the Revolutionaries and Bonapartists : " I had no other means of saving their country, their property and their lives." It is not so easy to understand the zeal with which Fouché at once began to serve the Bourbon régime. He had, however, many advocates amongst the foreign statesmen, above all the Duke of Wellington, and also the King's brother, the Comte d'Artois, joined in their recommendations. When, however, Louis XVIII consequently accepted Fouché as his Minister of Police he felt that he ought to veil his action under a tragi-comic exclamation: " Unfortunate brother ! If you saw me you would pardon me ! " Chateaubriand has given us a very vivid picture of the scene when Fouché took his oath of fealty to his new ruler in the presence of Talleyrand, the ex-Bishop of Autun, who had incited Napoleon to the murder of the Duc d'Enghien, and had now been appointed as the King's Prime Minister. " The proven regicide kneels and lays those hands of his, that had helped to behead Louis XVI, between the hands of the martyred King's brother, whilst the apostate Bishop stands by as sworn witness." When Fouché now became Minister of Police for the fourth time, the appointment was, perhaps, a prudent concession to a chance political emergency, but could scarcely be looked

P   225 upon as likely to prove permanent. To pass in this way from the hundred days' Empire to the Bourbon rule may, indeed, have seemed daring and defiant, but the gulf between Fouché's dark past and the brilliance of the " white reaction " was too great for any bridge to cross. To Fouché's honour we must, however, add that he was never in any way satisfied with the specious attitude of a professional politician, but remained a political fighter always ready to give battle, as far as opportunity allowed, in loyal defence of his old cause, the protection of the legacy of the Revolution.

Just as Fouché, on January 1, 1801, after the incident of the infernal machine, had a number of Jacobins deported in order to gain time in his contest against reaction, so now he was compelled to stoop to the drawing up of proscription lists against those Revolutionaries and Bonapartists who had particularly roused the Royalists' wrath. On July 24, 1815, it was consequently resolved, first, that eighteen generals should be court-martialled forthwith, and next that thirty-eight other persons should be kept under guard until the Assembly had decided as to their fate. Amongst the latter was Fouché's own old colleague, Carnot. The extraordinary part about this is that this measure, which branded Fouché as a traitor in the eyes of his former follower, was, from a tactical point of view, an essential step in the campaign against the ultra-reactionaries which the Minister of Police was now beginning. For he considered he had now put limits to the persecutions directed against the Left, whilst at the same time providing himself with a kind of " moral " starting-point in his feud with the Right.

So Fouché forthwith marched to the attack. On the one hand he tried to vie with the arch-reactionaries themselves in devotion to the Royalist cause by maintaining that it was Louis XVIII's wish that peace and reconciliation should reign between the different parties. On the other hand he insisted that his opponents on the Right broke the peace by persecuting former Bonapartists and Republicans. Apparently in the King's interests then, Fouché took everywhere the sharpest proceedings against the Royalist " rabble ". That by such open measures he, as a matter of fact, widened the gulf between the Bourbon followers and the other parties did not trouble him particularly. For in spite of his harmless manner Fouché clearly saw that internal divisions were the very breath of his political life, the one essential if he, with all his heavy load from the past, was to force his way forward in the teeth of a head wind.

Outwardly Fouché certainly advertised himself as an apostle of national unity. " Do not joke about the blockheads ", he wrote at this period, July 23, 1815, to one of his confidantes, Madame de Custine, " they are a power in critical times. According to them, to rule only means getting on in the world, indulging their lusts and shutting their eyes to the future. In my opinion it is to reconcile all parties, all differences of opinion, to the King, to bridle ambition and to lay all at the foot of the throne." Nevers and Lyons had quite sunk below the horizon !

A moment's pause was now granted to Fouché, an idyllic sunbeam rested on his narrow thorny path. The Royal House showed him unmistakable signs of its favour. On the recommendation of the Comte d'Artois, he was elected by the City of Paris as Deputy in the Second Chamber of the new House of Representatives. Louis XVIII himself deigned to witness Fouché's marriage certificate when, on August 1, 1815, he married again, this time a lady whose acquaintance he had made in his exile at Aix, Alphonsine-Gabrielle Ernestine de Castellane-Majastre, a lady in the middle twenties, second daughter of Henri-Augustin Alphonse, seigneur de Rians et de Tourves, chevalier de Malte. Fouché himself emphasized somewhat contemptuously to Barras that the family was poor. He evidently wished by this to counteract the idea that he had married above his station, and had allowed himself to be conquered by *l'ancien régime*, and that too in its feminine form. Nevertheless, it must not be forgotten that Fouché had for long been wheedling his way into many Royalist circles, and that he evidently still possessed that father confessor's scheming and persuasive influence over the heart of woman which, at an earlier date, had charmed Charlotte Robespierre. Three years had passed since he had lost his first wife, and he now longed to regain the quiet harbour of family life. Curious onlookers reported derisively that the fifty-six-year-old husband devoted himself to his charming wife with all a youth's glowing ardour.

But Nemesis was on the way. The majesty of the people's will to which Fouché had once offered such servile homage, but which he afterwards so unceremoniously restrained during Napoleon's time, was asserting itself again as passionately as before. But its wrath was now turned, not as in 1793 against the monarch, but against the men who once had cut the ties between the nation and its past. For the same election which had made Fouché a Deputy had sent to the House of the people's representatives a Royalist majority incomparably stronger both in numbers and fanaticism. Soon the country resounded with criticism of a ministry which counted amongst its members that Fouché who ought to have to content himself with " money and contempt " for his suspicious services.

Would Louis XVIII be able to stand out against this violent expression of opinion ? In any case Fouché thought it wise to try to get a more reliable backing. He, who lately had restrained Napoleon's arm in the midst of his blows against the enemies of France, now tried to speculate in patriotic feelings, and thereby to secure for himself a stronger hold upon the nation's confidence than before. His effort took the form of a memorial that Fouché presented in Council, protesting in patriotic indignation against the conduct of the foreign soldiers on French soil. Talleyrand, the Prime Minister, who was already revolving plans to get rid of his pretentious colleague, smiled scornfully at his juggling with high politics. Perhaps it is unjust though to ignore entirely the patriotic zeal that Fouché here displayed. Perhaps in his patriotic phrases there was an echo, even if but a distant one, of the general levy of the year 1793 and the mobilization in 1802 of the National Guard for the freedom of fair France. The foreign ministers, at all events, did not make much of Fouché's diatribe even after this had been secretly distributed far and wide. But although the head wind was strong, the Minister of Police still kept his course on the high seas. Talleyrand, who was afraid to meet the new House in Fouché's company, nevertheless failed in his attempts to get together a majority of the Ministry against him.

But the storm of adverse opinion continually increased in force. Two people were the final cause of Fouché's shipwreck, his own Police Prefect, Décazes, the hope of the " ultras " and a rising man, and above all the Duchesse d'Angoulême, who in September made her appearance in Paris society, and could not endure the sight of the old regicide. Then the Comte d'Artois entirely withdrew his favour from Fouché. " The justice of God became evident in his person ", says his biographer, Madelin. Divine patience had certainly been long-enduring. Never, moreover, had Fouché's contempt for humanity appeared in so plain and ruthless a guise as during this, his last period of office, when he, without more ado, adopted the view that everyone's politics were fundamentally nothing more than a competition for power and influence, in which the best-trained and most crafty must carry off the prize. In any case, one cannot but see the irony of the fact that it should be Talleyrand, Fouché's undoubted superior in depravity, who was to give him his death-blow. Talleyrand had offered him the post of Ambassador in the United States, but when this proved in vain, he said shortly, " I know a way to settle him." And on September 15, Fouché read in the Government newspaper the fatal notice that he had been appointed Louis XVIII's Minister in Dresden. Thus Talleyrand had at last got the upper hand in the long rivalry between them both. But he also was soon to have to retire into private life for the time being, as the shrewd

King Louis XVIII was glad to sacrifice him as the price of Czar Alexander's favour, of such value to him at that time.

But when the forces of reaction had thus swept away Fouché, it was destined that the cause which had been the deep passion of his life should still find a champion to save it from sharing his ruin. Manuel, the hope and legatee of the fallen politician, always struggled into the breaches which the Royalist salvos opened in the innermost positions of the Revolution. He, too, was afterwards to be got rid of by unscrupulous opponents and carried off by death before the hour of revenge could come. But behind him we already catch glimpses of other enthusiastic and earnest figures, Guizot and Thiers, those men of Liberal principles whose part it was to be to revive the traditions of the revolutionary Empire, and, whilst following in Fouché's footsteps, in their own time to make up for his frequent errors.

Chapter XXIII

Fouché's Exile and Death

In the autumn of 1815 Fouché went with his family to
take up his post of French Ambassador at the Court in
Dresden ; he was never again to see his own land, where
reaction was assuming ever more desperate forms, and
where Talleyrand soon had to hand over his office as
Prime Minister to the Duc de Richelieu. The Bonapartists and Republicans whom Fouché had betrayed the
preceding summer united with the Royalists in pouring
contempt upon his name and reputation. There was
no respect shown even to the amnesty which he had
received from Louis XVIII at the last change of Government, and, in a mood of fantastic excitement, the House,
in January 1816, passed a resolution that all " regicides "
who had held office during the " hundred days " should
be exiled from France for life. The King had not even
awaited this decision before dismissing his Ambassador
in Dresden. If Fouché had still kept his old liking
for satirical remarks, he would certainly have pointed
out how monotonously everything repeats itself. It was
now the turn of the Jacobin victims of unreasoning
public opinion to try the homeless existence of the
former émigrés.

But Fouché, old and worn out as he was, at this
juncture completely lost his head. He, who in earlier
times had so consistently maintained that the law of
expediency should hold unlimited sway in politics, began

232

to complain bitterly that his enemies had shown him no mercy, and thought more of his disastrous share in Louis XVI's death than of his many subsequent services to members of all the different camps. Or, as he wrote to Metternich on December 20, 1817 : "Is there not a single good deed by which a former error can be erased in governmental eyes ? " Fouché did not hesitate to sacrifice all his Jacobin principles if by doing so he could win favour with the great ones of the day. For example, in another letter to the Austrian Chancellor on June 10, 1816, he said, in speaking of the people : "Old customs, unchanging laws, a virtuous king are their constitution ; that is what assures them peace and pleasure, and forms life's true benefits." Where had his faith in the Revolution inheritance disappeared ? It vanished in smoke before the burning, desperate longing for power and influence which now drove on Fouché more fiercely even than in the restless days of his youth.

The least meditation must, of course, have reminded Fouché of the thought that lay at the root of all his policy during the summer of 1815, viz. that the Bourbons' rule was for the time being a necessity in France after all her desperate changes. He must, too, have surely seen how the present development, after so many excursions to the Left, was but the inevitable swing of the pendulum in the ultra-Royalist direction. The consciousness of the high offices he had filled, and the manly courage to preserve the dignity befitting his years, ought, moreover, to have combined in advising an attitude of reserve. It seems, too, that his clear understanding should at last have told him that he was now but a spent force, and that new times needed new men. If the principles for which he had striven embodied any living power, they would certainly come into fruition even though Fouché had left the scene of action.

All this may certainly be said, just as in any case it is easy for a moralist from his safe corner to pass a severe judgment on poor Fouché and his tortuous career. If we wish to try to understand both these we may find some help in the following words of Fleury de Chauboulon, Napoleon's spy on the Minister of Police during the " hundred days " : " Unfortunately his soul, blunted by the Revolution, has grown accustomed to and acquired a taste for great mental excitement; quiet wearies him. He requires unrest, dangers, revolutions. Hence this need for change, intrigue, conspiracy in fact, which has led Fouché astray into those errors which are so greatly to be regretted and so disastrous for his reputation." This is an objective observation which seems to provide a key to very much in Fouché's course of action. It was not only in the opinion of others that he was branded for ever as the regicide and the man who tortured Lyons ; the mental upheavals through which the actors in the French Revolution passed had also made a deep impression upon his very personality. But if this was the case, then Fouché's last days appear indeed in a tragic light, for, in their way, they reflect the fate of a whole generation.

It was to Austria that Fouché, in the summer of 1816, was compelled to flee for refuge. To begin with he and his family passed two years in Prague, where he experienced a good deal of annoyance from an old comrade in the times of the Convention, Thibaudeau,

234

who was amongst those proscribed on July 24, 1815. After a shorter stay in Karlsbad and Vienna, Fouché lived in Lenz until the new year of 1820; there a pleasant social intercourse brightened the exiles' life, and on festive occasions the Duchesse d'Otrante could be seen enjoying herself dancing to the strains of French horns and fiddles. But Fouché was constantly tormented by his unsatisfied craving for activity. The Ministry of Police loomed before his fancy as his entailed estate, which had been unjustly stolen from him, and he could not free himself from the oppressive idea that his genius for statecraft was indispensable in French politics.

Then with the new year of 1820 Fouché received permission to settle in Trieste, where, in the society of other exiles of high rank, Napoleon's sister and brother, Elisa and Jerôme, together with the latter's wife, Katarina, Princess of Würtemberg before her marriage, Fouché found rest and contentment.

Fouché, who during his exile had constantly threatened to publish his reminiscences, had in connection with this resolve allowed his thoughts to stray back from time to time to his first peaceful years in the Oratorian Order—to the Abbé Mérault de Moissy, who had at one time initiated him into the cool realms of meditation and permitted him to taste the sweetness of religious devotion. Perhaps there was also an undertone of seriousness in the lines which he wrote on March 3, 1819, to a comrade of earlier days, Eugène de Beauharnais: " Henceforward I am at the age when, if I do not exactly become a hermit, I am at any rate seriously thinking of preparing some credit for myself in another world whilst leaving a good example in this." But there is no doubt that Fouché's inborn scepticism and worldliness peep out too through these words. Just as before in his circular to the bishops in 1802, he still appeared to consider that religion was " an important matter akin to profane avocations," which might suitably be followed in its proper time and place.

In Trieste Fouché's spirit of unrest seems to have left him, and he became, instead, no more than a pleasant but outspoken and fascinating personage in society, so rich in experience of life and so attractive in his constant thoughtfulness for the welfare of his family and his friends. He no longer wasted his day with unnecessary and irritating desk-work, but, instead, regularly took his long, solitary walks. Then in December, illness came, caused by the harsh autumn climate, an obstinate inflammation of the lungs which foretold the inevitable end, whilst those around him followed its course with sorrow and anxiety. Oblivious now of revenge and intrigue, Fouché had his mighty records burnt by his bed, in which he had the active help of Jerôme Bonaparte. On December 26, at five a.m., Joseph Fouché, Duc d'Otrante, breathed his last sigh.

On December 28 his mortal remains were laid in the grave. That day Trieste was shaken by a snowstorm that, in its penetrating darkness and mighty force, seemed to re-echo the passions that had disturbed the life of the deceased. A gust of wind seized upon the hearse and overturned it in a moment. Long after, in 1875, his relatives had Fouché's body taken to Paris, where it now rests in the cemetery of Père Lachaise.

Fouché's wife, Alphonsine-Gabrielle, after his death, returned to France, where she was the constant object of her aristocratic relations' indignant disapproval, and where she remained a widow until her death in 1850. Fouché only had children by his first marriage, viz. his sons Joseph and Armand, who both died without issue, Athanase, Chamberlain to Oscar I of Sweden and ancestor of the present Swedish branch of the d'Otrantes, and also a daughter, Josephine, afterwards wife of le Comte de Thermes. Amongst his relatives and friends there was but one memory of Fouché, the fair record of a generous, warm-hearted and unforgetful man. Thus the historian, Léon Séché, in other respects Fouché's antagonist, has borne witness to the devotion and admiration that he inspired in his niece, Madame Riom, who with his sisters received from him all his possessions in Pellerin. These sympathetic traits do certainly form a part too of any portrayal of the Police Minister's character, even if it is true of him to an exceptional degree that his importance and his work secure him a place in history and bring him before its bar of judgment.

Chapter XXIV

The Verdict of Posterity

WHATEVER we may think of Joseph Fouché's conduct
during the changing scenes of his life, yet an inexhaustible
will-power, which only increased when faced with
difficulties, exceptionally penetrating intelligence, and a
political instinct which, it is true, could sometimes fail
him, but which in his fortunate moments was something
very like genius—these are the qualities that he shows
from time to time throughout his whole career. It has
been stated, but unjustly, that his one aim in all that
he did was his own advantage, and that he made a clever
use of all chances of advancement without ever risking
his position for a principle or cause. Certainly it is
difficult amongst his contemporaries to single out a
more unconscientious and unscrupulous intriguer than
Fouché himself, but we must also remember how persistently he worked to preserve the essential features of
the social state brought about by the Revolution and
consolidated under the Empire. If it is asked how this
contention can be compatible with such facts as that
Fouché, both in January 1801 and in August 1815, had
great numbers of Revolutionaries deported or exiled,
we may answer, first, that this was an emergency measure
taken in both cases to give Fouché breathing-space,
that he might afterwards, with all the more energy, take
up again the defence of the legacy left by the Revolution;
and, secondly, that this ice-cold man was never in his

political life accused of any private considerations. In his public work Fouché was, to an abnormal degree, organically free from either affection or personal animosity.

For first and foremost the fact stands out that he everywhere reveals his character as a practical politician, and if we seek a tangible symbol of Fouché's conception of the work of the Revolution, we find it in the national property confiscated from the Catholic Church and from the *émigrés*, to be afterwards, in great measure, distributed amongst the poorer classes of the people. Economic questions, speaking generally, claimed Fouché's attention at an early period. During the Terror he attacked them mercilessly in the equal distribution of property, the very symbol of communism. Later on, his programme changed in a very suspicious connection with the constant increase of his own private business interests. Thus in the Napoleonic period he was the champion of Industry and the Bourse. Everything was changed. The middle-class made their ostentatious entry upon the stage with promises of peace and reconciliation between nations in the industrial age. With keen and ready insight Fouché once more perceived the trend of the times and adapted himself to it. But the fate of the national property still continued to be his lodestar; to such a degree, at least, he was and remained a Jacobin during the Empire and the Restoration. It is but right to add that Fouché, in this respect, was not influenced by private economical interest of any importance. For his own extensive land property would have remained—if we may believe Madelin—practically untouched, in case the land which during the Revolution was wrested from the Church and the nobility had been taken and given back to its original owners. For Fouché is reported during the Napoleonic days to have come to an agreement with most of the former possessors of his property, which they declared fully satisfied all their claims from an economic point of view. It has been said, moreover, that the primitive instinct of self-preservation was from first to last the driving-force of Fouché's career. This, too, is probably only true with certain reservations. Certainly it should be stated much more emphatically than is usually done that Fouché during the Terror was the victim of pronounced forced convictions and was barely master of his own actions. The more closely we scrutinize his cold, reserved features and study his too perfunctory manner, the more we suspect that strong passions lie concealed behind this impenetrable exterior. But Fouché's instinct of self-preservation did not generally find expression as timidity or aversion to putting his own existence in danger. His attitude in the spring of 1810 and in the summer of 1815 gives proof of his courage, even though in later defeat Fouché did lose his self-possession. If, then, a consistent maintenance of certain political aims and personal courage cannot be denied to Fouché, there yet remains the objection to his mode of procedure that he preferred to carry out his schemes in the dark, carefully feeling his stealthy way along tortuous side-paths. The fact cannot be denied ; Fouché's public work entirely lacks that splendid valour, that bright light of publicity which lends lustre to the political career of a Guizot or a Gladstone. Fouché—as one author remarks—

undoubtedly had a certain "affinity with crime", a tendency to the immoral of an almost pathological nature. Yet this point of view is not quite decisive. A man who was to be of any weight at the side of such as Napoleon could scarcely make open assaults in defence of his ideas.

Apart from that, however, the problem of Fouché's character seems to be one of somewhat difficult solution. It is true there is no defence for a man who, after passing his youth in devotional exercises, later on revels in abuse of all religion, and at last, without inner conviction, ends by swearing allegiance to a Government which had an altar as its device. And the case against Fouché seems distinctly condemnatory when we also call to mind all the people whom he served and betrayed—the Girondists; his colleague in Nevers, Chaumette; his helper-in-need, the Vicomte Barras; his faithful ally, Josephine, and, last but worst of all, Napoleon and Louis XVIII! It is a long and eloquent list of his shots in political preserves! Who will say a kind word for a man with such a record?

Certainly no one. If all that was required had been simply to pronounce a moral judgment in this question, the matter would have been decided long since, and his biographer might spare himself long investigations that could only serve to satisfy an idle desire for sensation. Fouché, however, has undeniably occupied such a central place during so long and important a period of French history, that it is not only legitimate, but indeed highly requisite and useful, to study him from a political point of view as well. This has been the prevailing aim of the present book, and with this object in view it has been found of considerable service to follow his stormy career with special reference to well-known cases of his treachery. For it is remarkable that in scarcely any of these cases did he act from exclusively personal reasons—except possibly in his behaviour to Louis XVIII during the first Restoration. But otherwise, Fouché has scarcely ever betrayed the cause of his allies before they had become—when looked at from a political standpoint—antiquated and out of date. It must also be remembered that the risk of being dragged down too in their fall was by no means inconsiderable. Girondists went on blindly to ruin ; Barras, in his turn, during years of resentful insignificance had to expiate his political blunders. If Napoleon's Empire was not to be imperilled, the succession must be secured. But to do this, Josephine was doomed to lose her place in Napoleon's future history. And lastly, in reference to the latter's return to power during the " hundred days ", we must, indeed, acknowledge Fouché to have been right in his judgment that the existing state of affairs was a grave political mistake which tried the French nation to the uttermost, even though his political methods on this occasion, in all their Machiavellian perfection, end by filling us with aversion.

Allied with these historical notes is the question as to what Fouché, at these different junctures, was hoping to achieve by his " treacheries ". It is, of course, obvious that, eagerly as he worked in 1793 to widen the gulf between the opposing camps, in 1799 and onwards he endeavoured just as earnestly to arrange transitions from one system and government, to others of quite a different nature. It is also easy to find the one uniform distinctive

242

feature in all his aims and objects. In 1793 he united—in a disastrous way amid the excessive barbarity then prevailing—his destiny for ever with the revolutionary cause; later on, his one endeavour through all the changing scenes was, as far as possible, to preserve to his own advantage and that of all his accomplices and fellow-sufferers the principles of the Revolution from deterioration and bankruptcy. But this contrast in his outer history between 1793 and the period after 1799 is also apparent on his personal and psychic planes. On the one hand we find a political passion which does not shrink from any means to carry its ideals into effect, on the other we are surprised by a slippery adaptability, an ingenuity and a spirit of calculation which are without counterpart not only in his own time but possibly in any period of history whatever.

How can the self-contradiction in these last-named facts be explained?—for being, as it is, a purely psychological problem, it is more difficult to find its correct interpretation. Undoubtedly, like so much else in Fouché's history, it is a reflection of the process of the general human development then going on. The Revolution, that attempt on a large scale to translate theories into practice, had during its course brought with it terrible disappointments. At its close the election booths were, so to speak, strewn with shattered ideals. Enthusiasm had been changed into disillusion in the minds of the surviving politicians. Men's eyes were no longer fixed on the standards in their former contests, but their minds were chiefly occupied with their own personal advantage. It is true that Fouché formed an exception to this rule in so far that he, as

243

we have seen, still tried, when circumstances permitted, to serve the revolutionary cause; but who can blame him if the methods which he used were, to a certain degree, other than those of the Terrorist days ?

Further, it must be noticed that sharp as the contrast is between the Fouché of the Reign of Terror and the Fouché of the Napoleonic era, it is still not entirely irreconcilable. His biography shows, after 1808, an apparent relapse to his attitude of fifteen years earlier, a boundless self-confidence such as he showed in his dictatorship in Nevers and Lyons, and a recklessness in his schemes and intrigues that oversteps all bounds of moderation or reason. When Fouché, during Napoleon's absence, on his own responsibility calls out the National Guards through the length and breadth of the land, and when, without his ruler's knowledge, he treats of peace with England, do not his actions seem like those of a mere visionary, in very great measure comparable with the Jacobins' attempt to institute at one stroke a social state of perfect bliss ? And is not Fouché's whole policy during 1815, in spite of its masterly skill, just a balancing trick of the same unpractical nature ? We seem to find the key to all these enigmas when we perceive how Fouché, when his hour of failure had struck both in 1810 and 1815, falls into complete despondency and despair. Want of self-restraint in his conduct is thus, in reality, a sign of personal weakness, probably of a psychic nature—just as were his excesses during the political epidemic of 1793.

Fouché's poor reputation in the eyes of the world, if we consider the matter from an historical point of view, is due—as Madelin asserts—to the fact that at last he betrayed all political parties, that the Royalists taunted him with having " disgraced 1793 " by entering into Louis XVIII's service, and that the Bonapartists, Constitutionalists and Republicans could not forget that he had delivered them over to the Monarchy. All these complaints doubtless point to suspicious circumstances, but they are certainly not the last word concerning his political work. If, however, we look for the offence that has, more than all else, lowered him in the estimation of Frenchmen, we find it without any question in his behaviour towards Napoleon. How terribly Fouché's rough exhortation of " Let him go ! let him take himself off! or I'll have him arrested !" must grate in his fellow-countrymen's ears. The more Nationalism raises its head in France, the greater the fall in the Fouché shares— to use one of his own business-like expressions.

But in this, perhaps, we have at last found the very mainspring of Fouché's character, his profound lack of sympathy with the romantic and national movements which broke out during the nineteenth century, and which, although often evoked in the strife against Napoleon's despotic actions, were yet wont to look upon the conqueror's dreams of greatness and policy of power as the noblest models for their own efforts. In opposition to such opinions as these, Fouché appears, either voluntarily or from force of circumstances, as the upholder of pacifism, social welfare and democracy. As a matter of fact, he it is who thus handed on the ideas of the Revolution through the imperial era to the French civic government of the nineteenth century. With some justice he might have adopted for himself

245

one of Napoleon's half-sad, half-amused utterances:
" I am not a human being, I am an historic personage."

As regards ideals, Fouché cannot be named even in
a distant connection with, for example, such a man as
Lafayette, the dupe of democracy, but a childlike and
pure-hearted knight who always remained the same,
whether on the Bastille day in 1789 or by the barricades
of the July Revolution in 1830. For Fouché was a
corrupt being. But just because he was swept along by
the strongest current of the time and scorned no means
to keep himself afloat, his life becomes so indicative of
the course of events, and his personality so plainly
marked by the peculiar stamp of the environment in
which he had been educated and by the very many trials
through which he had passed.

It is through Fouché's work, therefore, that French
nineteenth-century democracy derives, from the struggles
and aspirations of the eighteenth century and of the
intellectual movement, its faith in individual happiness
and prosperity as both the moving force and the goal
of development. This was the vital aspiration to which
Fouché had once been trained by his pedagogic studies
in the Oratorian Order, and which ever afterwards formed
the atmosphere in which he lived. Fouché, moreover,
stands out as a politician of the eighteenth-century style,
both in his work as Minister of Police, stamped as it
was with the unprejudiced attitude of " the enlightened
despot ", and also in his intrigues woven after the classic
patterns of a cabinet diplomacy.

*   *   *   *   *

The slight, insignificant figure of the Oratorian and
his life, filled with unexampled storms, contests, mistakes,

remain to the very last a mystery, in spite of all efforts at solution. Michelet, the impassioned historian of the French Revolution, begins one of his descriptions on a personal note, which at this point we may well recall to mind. He explains that he had passed some winter months at Nantes ; in the thunder of the ocean storms and billows his mind dwelt on the terrible events and cruel settlements of the Reign of Terror, and, as in a vision, he felt he saw the play of elementary passions at this period of the history of France. Michelet's subjective method of investigation is here, as elsewhere, undoubtedly an example for both good and ill, but it is certain that as we follow Joseph Fouché, the sea captain's son from Pellerin, on his course between the sandbanks and breakers of his time, our minds now and again recall the words of the great French romanticist. And, as they do so, we are tempted to let Fouché's story end where it began—with a memory of the " toiler on the sea," who, sixty-one years before, had handed on to his son Joseph the torch of life.

Chapter XXV

Sources of Information Concerning Fouché

THE best and most complete description of Fouché's career is written by :

LOUIS MADELIN (*Fouché, 1759–1820*. Vols. I–II. Fifth Edition. Paris, 1923).

This is the book that has actually given rise to all the modern discussion on the Fouché problem. What is needed now is to find something between Madelin's original estimate of Fouché, marked as it is by a broad-minded but perhaps almost a too lenient view, and the frequently furious judgment of his opponents. Madelin's kindness to Fouché presupposes a certain amount of criticism of Napoleon. Yet Madelin, after the World War, gave utterance to a very high estimate of Napoleon in an excellent book, exceptionally well worth reading, entitled :

La France de l'Empire. Conférences prononcées à la Société des Conférences en 1926. Paris, 1926.

Anyone wishing to study the subject more thoroughly will find ample references to sources and literature in the preface and notes of Madelin's monumental work.

In addition the reader may note biographies by :

(*a*) CHARLES DUROZOIR (French historian, d. 1844), who has sketched Fouché's career very exhaustively. (MICHAUD. Biographie Universelle. XIV.)

248

(*b*) JEAN DE BRÉBISSON (*Fouché, Duc d'Otrante, Républicain, Impérialiste, Royaliste, 1759–1820.* Paris, 1906). The author in this has, in lecture form, quoted extracts from different sources, some of great interest.

(*c*) ALBERTO LUMBROSO (*Le "Portefeuille" inédit de Fouché de Nantes, Duc d'Otrante, Ministre de Napoléon Ier, Ambassadeur de Louis XVIII.* Rome, 1900).

(*d*) JOHN HOLLAND ROSE (in the *Encyclopædia Britannica.* Eleventh Edition).

Fouché has been treated from different aspects by :

(1) DE MARTEL (*Étude sur Fouché et sur le Communisme dans la Pratique en 1793.* I–II. Paris, 1873–1879).

(2) HANS VON HENTIG (*Fouché, ein Beitrag zur Technik der politischen Poliz in Nachrevolutionaren Zeiten.* Tübingen, 1919).

(3) EUGÈNE FORGUES (*Le Dossier Secret de Fouché, Juillet–Septembre 1815.* Paris, 1908).

(4) EDUARD WERTHEIMER (*Die Verbannten des Ersten Kaiserreichs.* Leipzig, 1897). An important contribution to Fouché's later history.

(5) A. BARDOUX (*Madame de Custine.* Études Sociales et Littéraires. Paris, 1898). (With several Fouché letters.)

Exhaustive studies in the form of essays have appeared, some written to controvert Madelin's interpretation, amongst others by :

(1) LÉONCE PINGAUD (*Fouché et Napoléon.* Revue des Deux Mondes, 1901, Bd. 6).

(2) LÉON SÉCHÉ (*Fouché de Nantes d'après un Livre Récent.* Revue Bleue, 1901).

(3) F. A. AULARD (" La Grande Encyclopédie ").

In addition to the above-named writings, to which I have given thorough comparative study, the following published documents have been particularly read :

(1) *Matériaux pour servir à la Vie Publique et Privée de Joseph Fouché dit le Duc d'Otrante.* Paris, 1821.

(2) ERNEST D'HAUTERIVE (*La Police Secrète du Premier Empire. Bulletins Quotidiens Adressés par Fouché à l'Empereur.* I, 1804–1805. II, 1805–1806. III, 1807–1808. Paris, 1908, 1913, 1923). And

(3) LÉON LECESTRE (*Lettres Inédites de Napoléon Ier.* I–II. Paris, 1897). In which the most important letters to Fouché are to be found.

In memoir-literature I have studied the two chief vindications of Fouché, written by himself :

(1) (*Notice sur le Duc d'Otrante.* Extraite et Traduite de l'Ouvrage Allemand, sous le Titre " Zeitgenossen." Leipzig, Amsterdam et Londres, 1816.)

(2) (*Correspondance du Duc d'Otrante avec le Duc de* . . . Leipzig, Amsterdam et Londres.)

And also :

(3) P. J. PROUDHON (*Commentaires sur les Mémoires de Fouché, suivis du Parallèle entre Napoléon et Wellington.* Manuscrits Inédits Publiés par Clément Rochel. Paris, 1900).

(4) FOUCHÉ'S so-called *Mémoires*, which to a certain extent have been revived by Madelin, have, of course, also been used. Swedish Edition, Stockholm, 1927.

Of great importance are :

(5) *Témoignages Historiques ou Quinze Ans de Haute Police sous Napoléon.* Par M. Desmarest, Chef de cette Partie pendant tout le Consulat et l'Empire. Paris, 1833.

Besides the above studies, incursions have also been made into the respective Memoirs of Barras, Barère, Bourrienne, Savary, Thibaudeau, Madame de Chastenay and others. As a guide through the literature dealing with the Revolution and the Napoleonic Era, use has been made throughout of the modern epitome by :

G. PARISET (*Lavisse, Histoire de France Contemporaine.* Bd. 2. *La Révolution 1792–1799.* Bd. 3. *Le Consulat et l'Empire.* Paris, 1920, 1921).

At different points digressions have also been made to the well-known works by SLOANE, MICHELET, THIERS, TAINE, QUINET, JAURÈS, DAUDET, VANDAL, SOREL, AULARD, FOURNIER and HOLLAND ROSE. Special works that have been more closely studied are :

(1) P. LALLEMAND (*Histoire de l'Education dans l'Ancien Oratoire de France.* Paris, 1888).

(2) F. BRUNETIÈRE (*Études Critiques sur l'Histoire de la Littérature Française.* Cinquième série, the article " De l'Idée de Progrès." Paris, 1896).

(3) F. A. AULARD (*Le Culte de la Raison et le Culte de l'Être Suprème, 1793–1794.* Paris, 1892).

(4) J. SINDRAL (*Talleyrand.* Vies des Hommes Illustres. Paris, 1926).

(5) SIR HENRY LYTTON BULWER (*Talleyrand.* Historical Characters. Vol. I, ed. 3. London, 1868).

(6) SIR DUNBAR PLUNKET BARTON (*Bernadotte and Napoleon*. London, Dublin, 1921). The last-named work is new, weighty and intelligent, and throws vivid light on Fouché's career.

(7) A. MATHIEZ (*Autour de Robespierre*. Paris, 1925).

(8) L. BARTHOU (*Le Neuf Thermidor*. Récits d'Autrefois. Paris, 1926). An excellent summary, with special reference to the part played by Fouché in this connection.

(9) J. BAINVILLE (*Le 18 Brumaire*. Récits d'Autrefois. Paris, 1923).

(10) E. DAUDET (*La Police et les Chouans sous le Consulat et l'Empire*. 1800–1815. Paris, 1895).

(11) G. GAUTHEROT (*Un Gentilhomme de Grand Chemin : Le Maréchal de Bourmont* (1773–1846). Paris, 1926).

(12) E. D'HAUTERIVE (*L'Enlèvement du Sénateur Clément de Ris*. Paris, 1926). Interesting from the fact that the author, the eminent French archivist, shows that in essential points he agrees with Madelin's estimate of Fouché.

(13) JEAN LOREDAN (*La Machine Infernale de la Rue Nicaise* (*3 Nivôse, An IX*). Paris, 1924). The two last-named books belong to the series Enigmes et Drames Judiciaires d'Autrefois.

(14) G. LENOTRE (*L'Affaire Perlet*. Drames Policiers. Paris, 1923).

(15) G. LENOTRE (*Tournebut, 1804–1809*. La Chouannerie Normande au Temps de l'Empire. Paris, 1923). The two last containing many documents.

(16) H. WELSCHINGER (*Le Duc d'Enghien*. L'Enlèvement d'Ettenheim et l'Exécution de Vincennes. Paris, 1913).

(17) L. PINGAUD (*Un Agent Secret sous le Révolution et l'Empire. Le Comte d'Antraigues.* Paris, 1898).

(18) P. COQUELLE (*Napoléon et l'Angleterre, 1803–1813.* Paris, 1893).

(19) E. GUILLON (*Les Complots Militaires sous le Consulat et l'Empire.* Paris, 1894).

(20) F. MASSON (*Sur Napoléon.* Paris, 1909).

(21) F. MASSON (*Joséphine Repudiée (1809–1814).* Paris, 1901).

(22) H. HOUSSAYE (*1815.* Paris, 1893).

(23) PIERRE DE LA GORCE (*La Restauration. Louis XVIII.* Paris, 1926).

And, lastly, mention must be made of the work which is a divining-rod indispensable to every Swedish reader who wishes to explore these historical fields, viz. :

HARALD HJÄRNE (*Revolutionen Och Napoleon. Några Drag Och Synpunkter.* Stockholm, 1911). A masterly collection of essays by H. Hjärne, Professor at Upsala University, unfortunately not yet translated into English.

The author of the present book has endeavoured, in his study of the above-mentioned writings, to found his presentation on the results of scientific scholarship and to arrive at the most unified and faithful interpretation possible of Fouché's political personality. Other sources to which the author has not had access have also been used by the writers mentioned above.

INDEX

INDEX